MW00464224

I REMEMBER

*Stories of a Combat Infantryman
in Italy, France & Germany
In World War II*

By

John B. Shirley

Copyright © 1993. 2005, 2009, 2013, 2017
by John B. Shirley

Printed 1993, 2005, 2009, 2013
by John Gordon at Camino Press

Reformatted and edited 2017
by Bruce Shore and Jean Shirley Otto

Distributed by *createspace.com*

All rights reserved. No part of this book may be reproduced in any form or by any means, electronic or mechanical, including photo-copying, recording or by any information storage and retrieval system, without written permission from the author, except for the inclusion of brief quotations in reviews.

John B. Shirley
jbshirley2017@gmail.com

CONTENTS

CONTENTS

1. Introduction

This collection of war stories first appeared in issues of the WATCH ON THE RHINE, the magazine of the Society of the Third Infantry Division. The first story appeared in 1978 and the last one in 1989. They were published in book form in 1993. Many veterans have lived through similar experiences, but have not recorded their experiences, and so appreciate seeing such stories in print.

I have only written stories that are well imprinted in my memory. They are first person stories that have remained with me over the years. Everyone sees a battle from his or her own perspective, and accounts vary. Only ten stories are included in this collection, because these are the only events I remember in detail, even though I was in and out of combat for over one year.

I was drafted into the army in March of 1943. I took my basic training at Camp Cooke, now Vandenburg Air Force Base, near Lompoc, CA. I was promoted to corporal at the end of infantry basic training, and assigned to the 166th Infantry Regiment at Fort Sill, OK. The regiment served as in-

Author in basic training at Camp Cooke, CA July, 1943

fantry school troops for the Artillery Officer Candidate School. In a few months I was promoted to sergeant, and in early 1944 was sent overseas as an infantry replacement. I sailed out of Newport News, Va. on a Liberty Ship with 500 other infantry replacements.

After twenty-two days at sea, we debarked from the ship at Palermo, Sicily. Trucks took us to Messina, a ferry across the Strait of Messina, and electric trains to Caserta, Italy. After a week in the 1st Replacement Depot near the Cassino Front, I was sent to Naples, and then to Anzio-Nettuno by LST (Landing Ship Tank). I was assigned to "I" Company, 15th Infantry Regiment, 3rd Infantry Division on the Anzio-Nettuno Beachhead. I was now an assistant squad leader in a rifle company with a few veterans of the fighting in North Africa, Sicily, Southern Italy, as well as three months on the Anzio-Nettuno Beachhead.

My platoon had many replacements with various lengths of service in the company. I did most of my fighting as a Tech. Sgt. serving as a Platoon Sergeant or Acting Platoon Leader. When I recovered from a wound and returned to my regiment I was given a battlefield commission to 2nd Lt. I was then assigned to "L" Co., 15th Infantry Rgt. It was a fine company, and during the occupation of Austria and Germany I served five months as a Platoon Leader, and two months as the Company Commander. I left

Europe in early December, 1945, and arrived home on Christmas Eve, 1945.

I received a Silver Star, two Bronze Stars with a V device for valor, a Purple Heart, and a European Theater Operation medal with six campaign stars and a Bronze Arrowhead for one invasion.

I was very fortunate to have lived through the war, and am pleased I can share some of my experiences with you.

John Shirley
Livermore, CA
September 2003

Acknowledgements

The photographs are taken from the *1947 History of the Third Division*, from the *Dragon Chronicle, The History of the 15th Infantry*, and from the author's personal albums

The statistics on WWII battle casualties are taken from a newsletter of the National Order of Battlefield Commissions

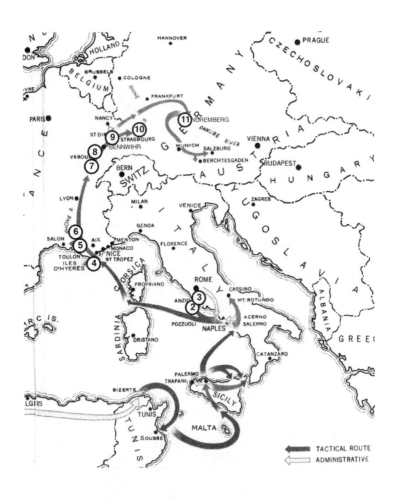

Battle route of Third Infantry Division. I joined the division campaign for the invasion of Anzio, just south of Rome. Encircled numbers reference the chapters that describe the action.

2. Into battle on a sled

Only one time in the history of the United States Army have steel sleds been used to carry infantrymen into battle. I rode on one of those sleds.

In April, 1944, as a buck sergeant with ten months of stateside experience in the army, I was assigned as a replacement to "I" Company, 15th Infantry Regiment of the Third Infantry Division, then fighting on the Anzio-Nettuno Beachhead.

The Third Division was one of the divisions assigned to attack out of the Anzio-Nettuno Beachhead near the end of May. The German Army had three and a half months to establish their defensive positions around the beachhead. They had extensive mine fields in front of deep anti-tank ditches. Barbed wire protected the minefields. There were hundreds of machine guns in a system of zigzag trenches, fortified houses, and deeply dug bunkers. The complete defensive line was over 1000 feet deep in front of our division.

German artillery and mortars were zeroed in on the fields we would have to cross. The beachhead was flat and featureless, and the Germans held the

Battle sleds were steel troop carriers pulled by a tank.

high ground all around the allied perimeter. The German soldiers in Italy were courageous, battle-wise, and had excellent commanders. It would be a formidable task to attack and overrun their positions. The day we would try it would be my first day in combat.

I was 19 years old. I welcomed the adventure and excitement, but I didn't want to die. I had strong feelings about duty, honor, and country, but I couldn't help wondering how I would react under

Practicing our battle-sled ride.

enemy fire for the first time. The Army calls it your "Baptism of Fire" and warns it can be terrifying.

The commanders as well as the foot soldiers were worried about the attack, and studied various tactics that might give us an advantage. One of the many ideas of our Division Commander, General John "Iron Mike" O'Daniel, would involve me.

His idea was to transport special assault teams forward on low sleds pulled along the ground by medium tanks. This was designed to move men forward quickly and with better cover than they would have on their feet behind tanks. The teams

A nurse digging a foxhole. On the Anzio-Nettuno beachhead no place was safe from German artillery, and everyone lived in foxholes. Hospitals are always located in the safest place possible. At Anzio-Nettuno, there was no safe place for the hospitals. In the four months the beachhead existed, the following medical personal casualties occurred: 82 killed in action, 387 wounded, 19 captured, and 60 reported missing in action.

were to become known as Battle Sled Teams, and each of the three rifle regiments in the division organized and contributed a team to this effort.

There were five 12-man squads in each sled team. Each sled was just deep enough and long enough for one man. The division ordnance company fashioned the sleds out of 3/16 inch steel plate, which gave some protection against bullets and shell fragments from the front and side, but no protection from directly overhead. Six sleds were placed end to end, and flexibly joined so the line of sleds would move in a snake-like fashion. Two parallel lines of six sleds joined together by steel rods in six locations along the lines of sleds would slide along the ground in the tracks made by the tank pulling them. The 12 sleds behind each tank would carry one squad. The squad leader could talk to the tank commander through a phone hook-up. Five tanks and their crews and 60 infantrymen in their sleds made up each Regimental Battle Sled Team.

Each Regimental Commander assigned 60 men to temporary duty with the sled team under his command. Each team had five sergeants for squad leaders, and five sergeants or corporals for assistant squad leaders. A First Lieutenant was assigned as Sled Team Commander. There were very few volunteers, so the Regimental Commander directed each of his nine Rifle Company Commanders to assign one or two sergeants, and several riflemen to special duty with the battle sleds. A Company Commander ordered to give up a sergeant and a few men for such an unusual and untried assignment is not going to send his best men. I was untested in battle, and was one of two sergeants detailed from "I" Company along with four privates

11

The men assigned to the battle sleds ate and lived with their company, and every morning for about three weeks marched off to a special training area. Everyone on the beachhead lived in dugouts because German artillery could cover the entire beachhead. Our sled team could train with relative safety in the rear areas, because giant smoke-fog generators laid down huge smoke screens along the front to obscure the vision of the German artillery observers.

German air and artillery still raised havoc with the rear areas. Hospitals would be located in the safest places possible. On the beachhead several hundred hospital personal were killed or wounded. The first six women killed in the European Theater were nurses on the beachhead. The first four women to receive Silver Stars in the war were nurses on the beachhead.

Occasionally shells interrupted the training, and once a man near me was hit with a small shell fragment. Anticipated objectives were laid out with white tape, and we rehearsed attack after attack. The sled teams had several weapons not generally assigned to infantry. One man was trained to use a flame-thrower. Another man carried a short tube of high explosive called a "Bangalore torpedo" to blow up barbed wire obstacles. Another man carried "satchel charges", which were small bags of high explosives to be placed against a bunker, or building, to blow it in. Since we were to attack "strong points", most of our fighting would be at short range. Most of us turned in our M-1 rifles for Thompson sub-machine guns, and we carried extra hand grenades.

After several weeks of training, utilizing our sleds and tanks, we became a team. At least, we charged the imaginary targets with enough enthusiasm and accuracy to satisfy our commanders. General Mark Clark, 5th Army Commander, paid us a visit one day to see the "Battle Sleds" operate.

Headquarters tried, without success, to keep our sled teams a secret from German intelligence. One evening, Axis Sally, an English speaking German woman who broadcast popular music, news of German victories, and other propaganda, had an announcement for those who had radio receivers. She told us if we tried to use the sled teams, we would be annihilated. Since we expected a difficult time at best, her threat added little to the anxiety we already were experiencing.

At the end of May the weather was balmy and beautiful as long lines of infantry formed to begin the march to the front. Just as dusk fell, and while we waited to start our march, mail call was held. Because of my long trip from the United States to Italy, my mail had not caught up with me. As it grew too dark to read, I received my first mail in three months. The mail clerk handed me 40 letters from family and friends. As we marched, I carried those 40 unopened letters in my pack, and wondered if I would stay alive long enough to read my precious mail.

The day we broke out of the Anzio-Nettuno Beachhead, May 23, 1944, was one of the worst single days of fighting any U. S. Army division endured. 995 Third Division men were killed or wounded in a very short time. The next day another 625 men met the same fate. Twelve days after the breakout, we entered Rome, and had 3,300 killed and wounded in our division in those twelve days.

On the morning of the attack the darkened sky was choked with smoke, dust, and the acrid odor of cordite from thousands of artillery and bomb explosions.

Our team was assembled in a house near the front. The men waited inside, and the tanks and sleds were camouflaged in the nearby yard. I heard the ungodly sounds of battle growing in intensity, and we were all thankful we were being spared, even if only for a few hours. If the assault companies were successful, perhaps we wouldn't be called.

*One of two 380mm German railway guns abandoned by the
enemy in the battle of Montelimar. This is like the guns used
by the Germans to shell the Anzio-Nettumo beachhead.*

Several hours after the attack started, a radio message called us to battle. The squad leaders met over
a map with the lieutenant. After a minute or two we
were waved towards our sleds without a word about
our objective. There was a great urgency to get
moving. I, as an assistant squad leader, didn't have
the slightest idea what we were expected to attack.

We lay on our stomachs, head down, in our sleds,
and moved onto the road and towards the front. We
couldn't see a thing with our heads down, and with
German artillery shells landing nearby, there wasn't
much inclination to look over the edge of the sled.
After a short distance on the road, the tanks made a

15

left turn into an open field. In what only seemed like three or four minutes, the tanks turned right and stopped. The squad leader yelled to get out and move forward.

We had stopped in a flat field of volunteer grain, probably wheat. As I climbed out of the sled, I kept a very low silhouette, as bursts of German machine gun bullets were chopping into the stalks of wheat only inches above my head.

As I lay on the ground next to the sled, I saw two wooden objects partially buried in the ground. They were right in front of me about 18 inches apart. A third one was just off my left heel. The objects were wooden anti-personnel Schu mines, buried by the Germans, but partially exposed by spring rains during the months of April and May. I was in a minefield. To move forward would be very dangerous. To stay next to the sleds would be even more dangerous. German artillery was starting to pound the area, promising to fulfill Axis Sally's prediction of annihilation. In a short while the sleds would be piles of junk.

In the field of grain, I could not see another person. I could tell where the battlefront was from the direction of the sound of the machine guns, and from the sound of bullets cracking over my head.

I carefully crawled around the two mines in front of me, and using an infantry crawl I was taught in basic training, I moved forward. I didn't see another mine, and I didn't detonate one. After 10 minutes I was still alive!

As I crawled about 100 feet, my body hugging the ground, I came upon a sight that was a great surprise, the edge of a wide and deep anti-tank ditch. Looking over the edge, I saw what was left of the 3rd Battalion, 15th Infantry, all crowded together in several hundred feet along the bottom of the ditch.

These were the survivors of the first hour and a half of battle from my own "I" Company, and what was left of "L" and "K" Companies. They had suffered heavy casualties, and were now taking cover in this deep ditch. As I scrambled down into the ditch, I realized the purpose of the sled team had failed. We had been deployed behind pinned-down infantry. What could a handful of us do that a half-strength infantry battalion couldn't do?

In combat when a commander is in trouble, he calls for all the help he can get, artillery, mortars, or whatever is available. In this case, it was the Battle Sled Team. The Sled Team objective was the fortified house, trenches, and machine guns just a short distance beyond the anti tank ditch.

Just after I arrived in the ditch I saw for the first time a man killed in battle. My "I" Company 3rd Platoon Sgt. tripped a booby-trapped land mine. He

17

was blown into the air about five feet, and came back down like a limp rag-doll. He had been a fine soldier and a veteran of North Africa, Sicily, Southern Italy, and four months on the Beachhead. If he could have lived 12 days, he would have been rotated back to the States.

The Battle Sled Team Commander was a good officer, and was committed to attempt to penetrate the German position to gain our objective. He gathered about him six of the sled team members he could recognize among the several hundred men all mingled together in the ditch. I was one of the six, and the other five were from my squad. He said we must do something, and asked me to look over the edge of the ditch towards the Germans to see what I could see. I moved down the ditch till I found a jagged break in the edge where a heavy artillery shell had blown part of the side of the ditch away on the German side. It was very difficult and frightening to lift my head up to see over the edge. As I looked, a huge puff of back smoke and fire exploded a short way in front of my face. The flame of the German flame-thrower stopped about 20 feet short of me. I only felt the heat. I quickly returned to the lieutenant to tell him about the flame-thrower and the broken trees, piles of rubble, broken buildings, and barren landscape in front of us.

As the lieutenant was trying to gather his team together and plan an attack, I saw a soldier crawl out of the ditch and head toward the German trenches. He was a member of my sled team squad we called "Flash". I didn't know much about him, as he was quiet and kept to himself. He was short and slight of build, with a sharp, thin nose. Most of us had short GI haircuts, but Flash wore his jet-black hair slicked down straight back over his head just as long as the Company Commander would allow. Flash had a definite lack of enthusiasm for army discipline and training, and had been known in "I" Company as an "eightball" or "goof-off". That is why he was sent to the sled team. Now Flash, without orders, was moving into action. Another rifleman followed him. I was next to crawl up the edge of the ditch. The Browning Automatic Rifleman (BAR man) from my squad followed me.

We crawled only a few feet when a bullet struck the man in front of me. I rolled him over, and saw his eyes were pulled up and set. He was dead. I crawled a few feet more and took cover behind a low pile of brick and rubble. The BAR man pulled alongside of me. I didn't know where Flash was, and no one else was behind us. About 20 feet in front of me was a zigzag trench. A dead German soldier was stretched out, face down, just behind the trench. What was left of a house was 25 feet to my right front.

I asked the BAR man to fire over the trench. With that fire as cover, I threw a hand grenade towards the door of the house. After it exploded, I sprinted into the room. It was empty. I stood in the cover of the door opening, and told the BAR man to cover me, as I ran the 10 or 12 feet to the German trench. Luckily, I jumped into a portion of the trench that was unoccupied. This trench made a turn every 10 to 15 feet. As I turned the corner of the trench, I found the next 10 feet empty. I moved cautiously forward, and found the trench made a 90 degree turn to the right. As I turned the corner, I saw a German rifleman firing to his front towards the anti-tank ditch. I fired a burst from my Tommy-gun into his back. I had just killed my first enemy soldier.

The trench made a 90-degree turn to the left. As I stepped around the corner I saw a German soldier behind a light machine gun. I fired a burst at him. After 3 or 4 bullets left my gun, the magazine was empty. I ran forward 10 or 12 feet, and hit him on his helmet with the butt of my Tommy-gun. I broke the wooden stock at its narrowest place. I kicked off the helmet, and struck him again with the metal part of the gun. He had probably been dead since my first bullets struck him. My movement to hit him was fast and automatic. When I looked over his machine gun, I could see men from the 3rd Battalion setting up a machine gun and others starting to climb out of the ditch and move forward. The attack was under way again, and I was worried they might not realize it was an American in the German trench.

I don't recall checking the machine gunner for a pistol, but as I moved back through the trench I checked the dead rifleman for a pistol. A pistol, especially a Luger, was a valued souvenir. The dead soldier probably had a pistol, but since the closed pistol holster, and the whole front of the soldier, was covered with blood, bright red and sticky, I gave up that opportunity for a souvenir.

I looked out of the outpost trench towards the main line of German trenches about 100 feet away, and saw something quite remarkable. Flash, all alone, was crawling toward the next German trench with complete disregard for his personal safety. He was about 20 feet from the German line when suddenly I saw five or six "Potato Mashers", as German hand grenades were known, come arching out of the German trench and fall around Flash. That was the last time I saw him. I am sure he was killed at that moment.

Just seconds after I saw Flash, and the "Potato Mashers", a small piece of white cloth appeared above the German trench. Then I saw another white cloth, then several pairs of arms appeared. Suddenly about 30 German infantryman stood up with their hands in the air. I was the nearest American to them. I waved them towards me, as I covered them with my broken, but reloaded, Tommy gun. Several of them were wounded. I moved them back into the anti-tank ditch that was nearly empty as the battalion was again on the attack. I passed near the "I" Company Commander. Our eyes met; no words were spoken, but there was an expression of admiration and gratitude on his face. For whatever motive he had for sending Flash and me to the sled team, I knew he was pleased with what we had done.

German mortar fire was now coming in on the fallen German position. This fire wounded one of the German prisoners. As the men of the sled team were scattered and our lieutenant killed, our fighting as a unit was ended. I was told by one of the officers to take the prisoners back to a prisoner collection point. I was to march the prisoners down the ditch and onto the road we had come up earlier in the sleds. Remembering the 3rd platoon sergeant who had hit a mine in that area of the ditch, I asked a big German Sergeant to lead the way. I warned him with the word "minen"(mine). He looked at me momentarily as if to say something. Then a tight, apprehensive look, with a slight smile, appeared. He nodded his head and moved forward. He went ahead of us about 25 feet lifting his legs high and setting his feet down gently. The Germans carried their wounded, some using blankets like stretchers. I felt sorry for the wounded, as some were in bad shape.

After I turned the prisoners over to some MPs, I returned to the house where we had waited earlier in the morning before our sleds moved up.

The "Sled Team" was considered dangerous duty, and it was. Flash, the real hero of our skirmish, was probably dead. Our lieutenant was dead, and probably many more. I had only seen five members of the sled team, all part of my squad, in the ditch. I don't even know what happened to the BAR man. I know what we had to endure wasn't as bad as what the rest of the companies had to go through. They were in the battle several hours before we got there, and when I left with the prisoners, they were still fighting. My first battle experience lasted a little less than two hours from the time we entered the sleds until I took the prisoners to the rear.

It would be two days before the German positions would be taken, Cisterna liberated, and the beachhead forces joined with the units of the Fifth Army fighting up from the Cassino front. It was early on the third day. Two French officers drove up in a Jeep to where my squad was located alongside a road. They got out and shook my hand. They were smiling, somewhat excited, and pleased they had made contact with the beachhead forces. I was pretty stoic, as I did not realize the significance of the meeting. GI's seldom know the big picture, but I should have been more aware of the reason for the joy of the French officers.

Since the sleds were destroyed, and most of the men of the team dead, wounded, or scattered, the few of us left in the house were sent back to our companies the next day.

Five days later I was the only sergeant left in the third platoon, and in command of what was left of the second and third platoons of "I" Company. The two platoons combined had 24 men where a week before the two platoons contained 80 of some of the best infantrymen in the Army.

On June 4th, we marched into Rome. I had only been in combat 12 days, but I was now a veteran. I had been through my "Baptism of Fire". Why I was spared to live where so many had died is part of the continuing mystery of life. I was lucky, I was grateful, and I was glad the first attack of the Battle Sled Team was also the last.

3. On the road to Rome

"For the want of a nail the shoe was lost. For the want of a shoe the horse was lost. For the want of a horse the battle was lost." Could the want of a horse mean the difference between victory and defeat in battle? Not likely, but small events do affect the outcome of battles. Did the explosion of a single artillery shell affect the outcome of an important WWII battle? Maybe.

The Third Infantry Division had just successfully broken out of the Anzio-Nettuno Beachhead after three bitter days of fighting, starting on May 23, 1944. Another day of combat resulted in the capture of Cori, Giuglianello, and a stretch of territory on the approach to Artena. Artena, some 20 miles south of Rome was a key town near Highway 6, and in German hands would protect their retreat from the Cassino Front. In our hands it would help us cut Highway 6. Artena was an important objective for the Third Infantry Division.

On the approach to Giuglianello, the division was moving over a two lane mountain road, all bunched up with trucks, jeeps, bumper to bumper, and long lines of infantry moving north. Four P-47's flew right over our 3rd Battalion a hundred feet above us. They started strafing after they flew over us, and hit the 2nd Battalion very hard, with about 35 soldiers killed and 70 wounded. We had yellow recognition panels on some of the vehicles, threw yellow smoke grenades, used to identify friendly forces, but to no avail. There were six giant German Tiger Tanks abandoned along side of the road, and I am sure the pilots thought we were German troops. It was a very tragic case of "friendly fire". The squadron was grounded for two weeks, and one of the pilots committed suicide.

My unit, "I" Company, was leading the 3rd Battalion, 15th Inf. Regt., as it marched into the small village of Giuglianello, five miles southwest of Artena. I was a newly acting Platoon Sergeant in the Third Platoon. As we rested in the center of town, a long convoy of trucks rushed in and rumbled to a stop. The town's main street was filled with vehicles. There was an urgency to get the 15th Infantry aboard the trucks, and on their way to Artena.

Infantrymen get very tired of walking, but they would rather walk than ride a truck near the front in broad daylight. Trucks attract enemy artillery and airplanes. On a truck you are bunched together. When you are on foot, you keep a 10 to 20 foot interval between men. When you are on the ground you are always looking for cover in the event of a sudden attack from artillery, small arms fire, or an occasional enemy airplane, and you can quickly dive for cover.

With some apprehension, we followed brisk orders to "load up". "I" Company was in the lead, and the 19 men of my 3rd platoon climbed aboard the first truck in the convoy. The day before, I had been made acting Platoon Sergeant. I was a buck Sergeant, and only four days before that I had seen my first combat as an Assistant Squad Leader, when we made our first attack on the Anzio-Nettuno Breakout. Now, a corporal and I were the only non-commissioned officers (NCOs) left in the platoon of 19 men. Since I was acting Platoon Sergeant, I climbed into the truck cab, and settled into the right seat. Rank has its privileges! The seat was much better than standing on the open bed of the truck. My newfound privilege lasted only two minutes. No sooner had I settled into the seat, than a Quartermaster Staff Sergeant appeared at the door of the truck. He informed me the Quartermaster furnished the trucks and he was in charge of the convoy, and since this was the lead truck, I was sitting in his seat. With a tinge of disappointment, I gathered up my rifle and pack, and climbed into the back of the truck with the rest of the platoon.

Fifty feet in front of our truck was a jeep leading the convoy, and was occupied by the driver and two lieutenants from battalion headquarters. We were headed for the town of Artena. Artena was supposed to be unoccupied, and we were rushing to beat the Germans to this strategic location. The truck convoy started to move, as one truck at a time raced from the cover of the buildings of Giuglianello. The trucks moved 50-55 miles an hour, and kept about 200-foot intervals. We moved along a winding mountain road, and came to a fairly long straight stretch of road in a little valley that ended in the low hills surrounding Artena. The drivers were as concerned for their lives, as we were for ours. We were most concerned about artillery. So far, so good.

When we were about two miles from Artena, without the usual whine or shriek of an artillery shell, a high velocity shell, probably an 88mm, exploded on the right shoulder of the road a few feet in front of our truck. Shell fragments, rocks, dirt, and a rush of hot air engulfed our truck, as it swerved to an abrupt stop on the shoulder on the right side of the road. The Quartermaster Sergeant was dead, having been nearly decapitated, the driver was badly wounded, and both lieutenants in the jeep were wounded, and so were three men from my platoon, one with severe abdominal wounds. While I was helping the soldier with the bad stomach wounds, everyone else, including the other two wounded soldiers left the truck and ran for cover in the deep gully 50 feet from the road. From the bed of the truck I looked back, and could see all of the trucks had stopped, and all the men of the 3rd Battalion, 15th Inf. were running towards cover from an expected artillery barrage.

One shell had stopped our convoy, and now German gunners could reap their grim harvest, but that didn't happen. Whoever fired the 88 at us did not risk another shot. One shell burst has caused our battalion to take cover two miles short of our objective. It would take the Company officers the better part of an hour to gather the companies, and get them on the road for a forced march to Artena.

By the time we entered the southern end of Artena, we had been delayed two hours. The column halted outside of the village. Since Artena was supposed to be unoccupied, two of our company officers, and two sergeants, moved forward to reconnoiter and plan for our company's deployment. As they rounded the corner of a building, probably with less caution than if they had expected the town to be occupied, they came into view of a German gunner on a flack wagon. Artena was not unoccupied! The Germans allowed them to move forward on the street until they were fairly exposed, and then opened fire. Two officers fell to the ground dead. One of the sergeants was killed, and the other wounded. "I" Company was now commanded by its only remaining officer, 2nd Lt. John Tominac. I was now given command of what was left of the Second Platoon, eight men, to join the 16 men in the Third Platoon. I had 24 men where, a few days before, there were 80 men in the two platoons, each platoon with an officer in command and a full complement of NCOs. Such was the devastating toll inflicted upon us by the enemy in five days of combat.

As we waited on a hillside outside of Artena, we looked down into the Artena Gap. Here we saw a remarkable battle unfold. Defending the Gap were units of the Hermann Goering Panzer Division. Attacking them was a Combat Command of the 1st Armored Division, US Army. Also in the attack was the 7th Infantry Regiment of our Division. In support of our attack were 20 battalions of artillery. We watched the tanks maneuver against each other, and saw the explosions of the artillery and tank shells. As it grew dark, the battle continued, and the explosions were more vivid in the darkness. The Germans held the Gap and eventually that attack was called off.

"I" Company was now very weak and we were placed in a defensive position on the crest of a mountain on the Division's right flank south of

Artena. It was from this position that I was ordered to take a reconnaissance patrol to scout out the mountains and a village to our South looking for Germans. I spent 15 hours on this patrol. No Germans were found, thank God, as we were often in very exposed terrain.

It would be four more days of hard fighting by the entire Third Division and the First Special Service Force, and units of the First Armored Division, before Artena was captured. The Herman Goering Panzer Division, an old adversary of the Third Division, made a gallant stand. On the fourth day, as we moved through Artena and onto low hills northeast of the village, we came upon a view everyone in the Fifth Army had been waiting to see since the Anzio-Nettuno landing. We stood on the crest of a hill, and saw, less than a half mile away, a long straight ribbon of highway, Highway 6, the road to Rome.

Had we trapped the retreating German Army? Hardly. Coming from the south, as fast as his motorcycle would go, was a lone German soldier. Several MI's fired, but in a moment, the German soldier was long gone on the road north to Rome. Had we seen the last German soldier out of the Cassino front? Perhaps. Did one well aimed 88mm shell keep us out of Artena at a strategic moment, allowing the Germans to occupy Artena for the defense

of Highway 6 to allow their retreat from Cassino?
Maybe, but we will never know. The Gods of War
aren't talking

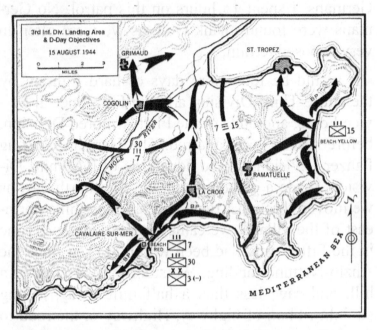

Landing area and objectives for 3rd Division, Cava-
lier-sur-Mer, France, August, 1944. "Beach Yellow" on
the East coast, is where I landed.

4. *Beachhead*

ANVIL, the invasion of Southern France, was easier than anyone expected. It was also one of the best planned and executed amphibious landings of the war.

It was my fate to participate in that invasion. Our battalion, aboard a navy Attack Personnel Transport, moved out of Naples Harbor on August 12, 1944, and joined a convoy of similar transports. I stood at the ship's rail looking at the sights in the harbor, and counted nine hospital ships. Although I didn't see him, Winston Churchill, I learned later, had moved about the harbor that day on a small craft waving his famous "victory" greeting at passing ships.

We sailed north past Corsica, and arrived off the coast of Mediterranean France in the dark morning hours of Aug. 15th, D-Day. H-Hour would be 8 a.m. The Third Infantry Division had made night landings in North Africa, Sicily, and Anzio-Nettuno. This was to be its first daylight invasion.

Each soldier dealt with fear and anxiety in his own quiet way. We left our bunks and lined up for coffee and our last meal aboard ship, courtesy of the U. S. Navy.

At 6 a.m. we were on deck dressed in woolen O.D.'s (Olive Drabs), combat boots, and loaded with our gear including M1 rifle, helmet, field pack, gas mask, ammo belt, canteen, entrenching tool, bayonet, C rations, extra bandoleers of ammunitions, and extra hand grenades for most infantrymen. Some were armed with Browning Automatic Rifles, pistols, and carbines. Others carried bazookas and bazooka ammunition, light machine guns, machine gun ammunition, light mortars, and mortar shells.

Thus heavily loaded, we climbed over the ship's gunwales down cargo nets hanging along the ship's side. The cargo nets served us like rope ladders. We placed our hands and feet on the rope very carefully, because to fall, loaded as we were, was to sink to the bottom of the Mediterranean Sea. As we neared the water, we could see the landing craft bob up and down, in and out against the ship. The trick was to let go of the cargo net, as the craft moved up towards you, keeping all your gear with you, find the thin rail side with your foot, then jump the four or five feet to the deck of the bucking craft. We had practiced several mock invasions off the coast of

Italy, so the experience wasn't new, just difficult and frightening.

Our LCVP (Landing Craft-Vehicle Personnel) pulled away from the mother ship, and joined a group of similar craft circling about two miles off shore. We circled while all the landing craft were loaded and maneuvered into positions that would deliver platoons, companies, and battalions to their proper beaches. As we circled in the early daylight, we could see the hundreds of ships that formed the invasion armada. In every practice invasion I had become very seasick within 20 minutes after entering the LCVP. My helmet served as a catch basin after I became nauseated. On this day, however, fear, anxiety, excitement, or something, kept me from being seasick. It was a pleasant surprise, and a small plus to what would be a long, difficult day. After about an hour, and a little more of circling, the landing craft moved out of the holding pattern, and lined up abreast for the dash to the beach.

The warships from the British, French, Dutch, and United States navies softened the beach defenses with everything from 16 inch shells fired from battleships, to small rockets fired from landing craft. In our practice landings in Italy, several times we had to wade ashore in chest deep water. On this landing our LCVP ran up on the sandy shore and we stayed dry, as we stormed the beach that Bridget

Bardot has since made famous. Saint-Tropez, now famous for Bardot and nude and topless bathing, meant nothing to us then. Our battalion's segment was designated "Beach Yellow". I doubt if anyone in our platoon knew the code name, but it was a poor choice of words. We were scared, but we were not "yellow".

I was a Squad Leader in the Third Platoon, "I" Company. When the front of the landing craft dropped, I led my squad over the soft sand for about 60 yards to a ditch on the edge of a coastal road where we took cover from enemy fire coming from a hill to our front. My squad reached the road without a casualty. If there were mines buried in the sand, we missed them. Our platoon was ordered to attack up the hill where the Germans were resisting our advance. Light machine guns and riflemen from another platoon put down a base of heavy fire toward the German positions, as we formed a skirmish line along the road. It would be dangerous attacking up the hill covered with trees and low scrub brush. We couldn't see our enemy, but we knew he was on the hill in front of us. Under orders of company officers, we left our cover, and started up the hill firing our rifles towards the enemy positions as we moved forward. Because of our training and discipline, we moved out without much thought of the consequences. It was a little unreal, more like a training exercise. Germans fired rifles at us, and men were hit on both sides of me. A half-hour later, we stood on the crest of the hill. We had driven the Germans out of their position. Several Germans were killed, as they tried to escape down the backside of the hill. My 12-man squad on the beach was now a seven-man squad. One man had been killed, and four were wounded. Nearly fifty percent casualties in less than an hour was a high price, but we had broken a thin crust of resistance, and, fortunately, did not have another fire fight the rest of the day.

Our platoon joined the Third Battalion Battle Patrol, and spent the next seven hours looking for enemy soldiers in the coastal gun emplacements that dotted the St. Tropez Peninsula. The few enemies we found were taken without a fight.

About 6:30 p.m. we sat down by a small stream, washed our feet, changed socks, and ate a can of C rations. After resting for about a half-hour, we started marching. We marched all night with five to ten minute breaks every hour. We marched all the next morning, and finally dug in at 4 p.m. near Brignoles. We had covered about 35 miles, and had been up 36 hours fighting, scouting, hiking, and sweating under the hot sun, as we marched up and down the hilly coastal roads of Southern France. Our march was especially hard on flank patrols, as they had to keep up with the main body while scouting out the hilly brush and forestland adjacent to the road. My squad took its turn on flank patrol. At one spot we walked right up to the muzzle of a light machine gun pointed at us. The gun was well hidden in the brush. A German soldier was lying prone behind the gun. He was alone, and, mercifully, surrendered without taking our lives, which he could have easily done. He wanted to live as much as we did, and surrender was his safest alternative.

General Patch, Seventh Army Commander, was directing the invasion. He had expected more difficulty, and planned to build up supplies and forces before moving too far inland. The formidable 19th German Army was assigned to defend Southern France. It was a strong, capable force, and could have caused an overextended 7th U.S. Army a lot of trouble. What were the German's intentions? Would its 19th Army make a stand? Soldiers on the front don't know the "big picture". The generals hope they do, and this time General Patch really did.

Instead of waiting for supplies and support as he had planned, the general kept us moving west and inland at a rapid rate. General Patch knew something only three or four persons in the 7th Army knew. On D+2, ULTRA, the super-secret code-breaking intelligence organization had intercepted Hitler's radio message ordering the 19th German Army to withdraw from Southern France. Col.

Donald Bussy was 7th Army's ULTRA representative.

When he took the D+2 intercept to the 7th Army's G-2, Chief of Staff, and General Patch, the general remembers that being "the nicest news that we ever heard."

With this knowledge, General Patch sent all elements of the 7th Army north on one of the most rapid advances any army made in WWII, fighting German rear guard actions all the way. The supply effort was heroic, and we were never short of C rations and rifle ammunition. The Germans fought a very effective rear guard action, and provided us with one firefight after another. At Montelimar, the German 19th Army was almost trapped. While most of the personnel escaped, a lot of their heavy equipment was destroyed.

The French people welcomed us warmly, as we liberated one town after another. The village bakeries were occasionally among our first objectives. The bread was delicious, and we emptied a few of the bakeries on our route. The civilians offered wine, and occasionally a piano was rolled out on the sidewalk to serenade us as we marched down the main street. We helped ourselves to some of the fruit, vegetables, and eggs from farms and gardens, but looting was strictly forbidden.

On September 13th we captured Vesoul. St. Tropez to Vesoul, in a straight line, is 400 miles. In less than one month we had traveled more than 400 miles in by no means a straight line as we maneuvered against the German rear guard. At the end of September, German resistance stiffened as we approached the western foothills of the Vosges Mountains. The Vosges Mountains guarded the route into Germany and had never been crossed in modern times by a military force opposed by an enemy.

The invasion of Southern France was over. The invasion of Germany was ahead, but first we had to cross the Vosges Mountains. Could we cross this "impassable" barrier? Yes, we crossed it at great cost, but that is another story.

5. Patrol

"Never volunteer" was advice most infantrymen followed. Occasionally soldiers volunteered for a patrol, but it was patrolling most G.I.s would avoid if possible. In WWII combat, patrolling meant a variety of activities, all dangerous.

Flank patrols scout terrain adjacent to the main body's route of march. Keeping up can be very difficult, as the main body usually moves on improved roads, and the flank patrol is working its way through forest, meadows, and scrub often on hillsides that have a lot of up and down terrain, gullies, etc.

Contact patrols are usually a few men working their way back and forth between two adjacent defensive positions that have some separation between them. If the distance is very great, the patrol's activity is very important in scouting possible enemy penetration or flanking activity.

The most common patrol, the recon-patrol, is reconnaissance and intelligence gathering. The patrols are assigned specific terrain to scout. Their task is to learn as much as possible about the enemy, and they are often asked to capture a prisoner. Such patrols avoid detection and combat if possible.

A combat patrol is usually a platoon to company in size, often reinforced with light machine gun and light mortar squads. Their objective is to engage the enemy in a firefight to determine the opponent's position and strength. Sometimes they are asked to capture and hold certain territory as long as possible.

The longer an infantryman is in combat, the more patrols he will experience. I had my share. Shortly after making the landing in Southern France, my platoon was assigned a light machine gun and a light mortar squad, and was sent on a combat patrol toward German lines that were the very outer defenses surrounding Marseilles. The First French Army was given Marseilles as their objective, but the Third Infantry Division fought to the outskirts.

The day before we reached the hills surrounding Marseilles we were riding on tanks and tank destroyers to make better time. We moved rapidly and unopposed on the main coastal road towards Marseilles. The TD (Tank Destroyer) I was riding was moving fairly fast when we saw alongside the road a lone black soldier dressed in the uniform of French Colonial Infantry. He wore cotton olive drab, old-fashioned leggings, a campaign hat, and no helmet. His rifle was an old Enfield. He had been separated from his unit, and spoke no English. We motioned him to climb aboard. He had a kind face, a gentle demeanor, was about six feet tall, and about 30 years of age. We assigned him to the weapons platoon, and gave him machine gun ammunition to carry. His machine gun squad was the one assigned to our patrol, and that is how a French Colonial Infantryman soldiered with us.

Our Lieutenant led the patrol as we climbed the moderately gentle, red granite, treeless slope of a low mountain. We hiked and climbed for nearly eight miles before reaching our objective at the summit. But just before reaching the summit, we came upon concrete and masonry gun emplacements and communication trenches, which were formidable fortifications. We were in these fortifications before we knew they were there. There was no barbed wire, no mines, and no Germans. If the position had ever been occupied, it was only for a very short period of time. The system was very new, and the absence of any kind of litter indicated it had never been used. We were lucky, for the gun emplacements had broad, clear fields of fire down the hill we had just climbed.

Our patrol moved through the position, and pushed to the crest of the low, broad mountaintop. We looked over the crest into a narrow valley directly below us. The mountain dropped off in a steep cliff about 150 feet nearly straight down. At the foot of the cliff was a road and a small village of about 10 or 12 buildings. Across the road was a fairly large cemetery surrounded by a low white plaster wall. On the road were parked about six passenger cars, and three or four trucks. Alongside a small refreshment stand stood about 20 German infantrymen drinking from bottles, probably water or soft drinks. A water wagon, driven by a German soldier, pulled by two large draft horses, was moving on the road. Other Germans were resting against the cemetery wall. One man was sitting on the seat of an outhouse with the door open and his pants down. Others were milling about the cars and trucks. All in all, about 150 soldiers were ready to move out.

We all took firing positions behind rocks at the top of the cliff trying to find positions that offered protection from counter fire. The French Colonial only had 13 rounds of ammunition for his rifle, and our ammunition wouldn't fit it. He chose his firing position very carefully, so he could make the most of his 13 bullets. He was on my immediate left on a small ledge four feet down the side of the cliff facing the Germans. He kneeled behind a small bush that offered concealment, but no protection from German bullets. He had the best field of fire of all of us. We all picked out targets. The man on the water wagon, and the man in the outhouse, didn't have a chance. When the first mortar round left the tube, we opened up on the hapless Germans who were killed and wounded in great numbers, as our rain of fire caught them by complete surprise. We fired our semi-automatic M1 rifles as fast as we could. The French Colonial took careful, deliberate aim as he squeezed off 13 shots. The next day we learned we had killed and wounded about 40 enemy soldiers. We left the mountain by the same route we used earlier in the morning. We had completed our patrol, and all the firing had been in one direction.

If the Germans had been occupying the trench and gun emplacements we found earlier in the day, a rain of fire would have hit us, and we would have suffered heavy casualties. It had been a combat patrol by definition, but not one bullet was fired in our direction. If we had only known, we could have volunteered!

*Author on right with friends in Naples after
liberation of Rome June, 1944*

6. *Fire three tracers*

The German 19th Army fought a very skillful rearguard action, as they withdrew their forces from Southern France in August and September, 1944. The American 7th Army made rapid progress as it moved North against the Germans, but not without numerous fire fights and skirmishes.

I vividly remember an incident that started at dusk about 10 days after our landing at St. Tropez. "I" Company advanced to the edge of a small village and was engaged in a brisk firefight. My platoon was in company reserve and was not engaged in the fighting. We could hear the sounds of battle to our front as we took cover along the edge of the road. Soon Capt. Stuart, our Company Commander, called our Platoon Leader, John Tominac, forward. We were detailed to make a flanking movement through the forest on our right. By then it was dark, and the forest was pitch black. The only way we could keep in contact was by grabbing a piece of webbing or equipment on the man in front of us. Since we didn't know what was ahead, we tried to move as quietly as possible. There were about 25 men in the platoon, all trying to stay together as we climbed a moderately steep hill. We tried to place our boots down as softly as possible, but every step seemed to rattle a leaf or snap a twig. The whispered warning "quiet" went up and down the column. The sound of a twig snapping was excruciatingly loud in the still of the night. Any noise was dangerous. I thought we sounded like a herd of cattle, but I know everyone was doing his best to move quietly.

After about an hour we stopped for the night, and our platoon dug in on a round defensive perimeter. One man was awake in each slit trench as the night turned into day. I was a Squad Leader, but had no idea what we were supposed to have accomplished on our flanking movement of the night before. As the sun came out, our Platoon Leader moved us to a clearing on the hill where we could look down into a village. This village was several miles North, and East, of the village where the roadblock impeded our advance the evening before.

As we looked down at the village about two miles distant, we watched a German NCO, or officer, placing infantrymen in a defensive position on the southern edge of the small French community.
What really captured our attention was the road leading north from the village. On it we saw long columns of German soldiers and equipment moving

Soldiers of the 3rd Division move through Larnod-Dorines for their assault on Besançon.

north as rapidly as they could. We saw batteries of truck drawn and horse drawn artillery including the dreaded "88's", dozens of horse drawn wagons and carts, many trucks and cars, a few tanks, and what seemed like several regiments of marching infantrymen. The Germans had to be desperate to expose such bunched up units in the daylight. They presented a perfect target for our artillery or airplanes. We watched with fascination, as the long columns moved away from us. Our Platoon Leader had a walkie-talkie radio, but couldn't make contact with anyone. It was very frustrating to watch the best artillery target we had ever seen moving away

3rd Division infantrymen moving up near Schirmeck past a dead enemy soldier. We didn't always have to walk.

and
not be able to do anything about it. When the platoon leader realized he couldn't call for artillery, he sent a runner back the way we came with a message to send up a forward artillery observer. About noon the artillery observer and his radioman arrived. The

German column had long before moved out of sight.

The only target left were the German infantrymen dug in on the southern edge of the village. Soon they were taking a terrible pounding from our 155mm howitzers. We watch the barrage, and felt sorry for anyone having to undergo such an ordeal.

That evening, shortly after dark, the platoon leader detailed me, and five men from my squad, to patrol into the village. He was sure the Germans had left. He instructed me to take three tracer rounds, enter the village, and if all was clear, to fire the tracers into the air and wait until the platoon joined up with us. It would be an easy patrol if the Germans had withdrawn as we had expected.

Using a compass, taking back azimuths in case we had to return to the platoon's position, our patrol moved down the hill through a fairly dense forest. We came to the edge of a meadow about a half-mile from the village, moved to our right front, and intersected a road leading into the village from the south. We climbed a fence, and started moving north on a very muddy road. On both sides of the road were tall rows of large trees. Their canopies ran together high above the center of the road. It was like walking in a dark tunnel. The sky was clouded over, and rain fell intermittently. On the left side of the road where we were moving was a fairly tall, thick hedge.

With six men sloshing in the mud, the noise was much too loud for a safe approach into the village. I had four of the men wait, and a scout named Steele and I continued. We were able to move much more quietly. After a short while I thought I heard the faint rattle of mess gear to my left on the other side of the hedge. We were just about in the area where we watched the Germans dig in earlier that morning. I found a small opening in the hedge about two feet in diameter about waist high. I stuck my head and shoulders, along with my rifle, into the opening. I wanted to hear better, and to see what I could see. Just as I pushed my upper body into the opening in the hedge, with Steele standing at my immediate right, we heard the dreaded challenge "Halt, Halt". The German soldier who challenged us was not more than 20 feet away, as best as I could judge. He sounded as scared as we were. Steele and I froze in position not daring to make the slightest movement or sound. We could hear the German whisper to his companion. No doubt they were wondering what to do next.

After what seemed like several minutes, we could hear the Germans taking steps towards us. It sounded like one was on each side of the hedge. To fire at the sounds in the blackness of the night would have given away our position and strength. Our muzzle blasts would have made targets for them and their comrades. After the Germans had taken several steps, Steele, from the deepest recesses of his throat, whispered, "what shall we do?" I whispered back, "run for it". He turned, and I pulled myself out of the hedge, and we headed back the way we came. Almost immediately the Germans started firing at us. What saved us was the mud! To run was almost impossible. The mud grabbed our ankles and our forward momentum threw us face down into the muck. I must have fallen three or four times. The bullets missed because we were flat on our faces most of the time. About 10 to 15 bullets snapped above and around us without hitting either of us. Steele and I made it back to where the rest of the patrol was waiting.

They had heard the firing, but didn't know what to do. We were very glad to see each other. Following our compass back azimuth, we worked our way up the hill to where we thought the platoon was dug in. After a brief search we posted guards and slept till morning when we found the platoon less than 50 yards from where we stopped for the night. The Platoon Leader had heard the gun shots, and was glad we made it back.

Soon orders came for us to join up with our company. "I" Company bypassed the village my patrol had tried to enter. As our company moved north in pursuit of the Germans, I carried the three tracers in my pocket. I learned later it took units of the 2nd Battalion, 15th Infantry, another day to capture the village!

7. The rock quarry

Battles are often remembered, and named, for prominent terrain features. The battle of the Rock Quarry near Cleurie, France is such a battle.

The Cleurie Rock Quarry was used by the Germans as a main point of resistance as they developed their defenses on the western edge of the Vosges Mountains. The Vosges had never been crossed by any modern army opposed by an enemy. The relatively easy invasion of Southern France had carried the 7th U. S. Army to this formidable barrier.

The Third Infantry Division faced the German line of resistance on a broad front north of Remiremont. The men of the Third Division will long remember the difficult battles in the Cleurie, St. Ame, and Vagney Sector.

"I" Company was leading the Third Battalion of the 15th Infantry Regiment, as we first made contact with the enemy southeast of the quarry. I was Platoon Sergeant of the Third Platoon which was leading the company as we came down the Xatis-Halte-Bemont road early in the morning of September 27, 1944. We came out of the hills from the southeast and moved unopposed into a little valley with a few buildings at the Halte-Bemont crossroads.

Visibility was good, with none of the fog that occasionally caused us a problem. Our scouts were in the lead, followed by two spread-out columns, as we came down the road. We turned left at Halte. The road was two lanes and paved; still no contact with the Germans. There was a house on the right, about a quarter of a mile from the intersection, and that is where the fighting started for us. There was a slight curve in the road just before we reached the house.

Forty feet east of the house was a rock fence about four feet high, and our platoon took cover behind this wall. Two of the 3rd Squad's scouts entered the yard through a gate, as we covered them from the wall. They checked out two small buildings, both empty. Then they entered the rear door of a masonry, two-story house with a barn attached. Because there had been no resistance, the rest of the platoon followed the scouts into the kitchen in the back of the stone house. We surprised five or six German soldiers cooking breakfast. I don't think they had weapons in the kitchen, as there was no firing from them. I saw the last one run out of the kitchen towards the front of the house. I don't remember any of us shooting at them. It all happened so fast.

I looked out the front window and saw an empty dugout near the front door. Immediately a light machine gun opened up on the house. The machine gun was placed in such a way that it could fire only into the second story of the house. The house was just below a little knoll, and the Germans must have felt the high ground was the best place to dig in. In no time at all, the tracers had set the hay in the loft afire. Soon the building was burning rapidly. The French farmer and his wife started leading cattle out of the barn.

Fleeing the burning house we took cover behind the rock wall where we had covered our two scouts. The house protected us from direct German fire. We couldn't see their positions, and I doubt if they could see us. Since our platoon was about half strength, and without supporting weapons, our Platoon Leader ordered us to withdraw back along the road towards Halte. The first part of the platoon got back around the curve and to safety. The second half attracted German machine gun fire, and several men were wounded, and one man was killed. I hadn't left the wall when the machine gun opened up on the road. A BAR man and I were the only members of the platoon still behind the wall. I took the BAR, and started firing towards the sound of the machine gun on the far side of the house, even though I couldn't see its position. Fortunately, the machine gun stopped firing. The BAR man and I hesitated to expose ourselves along the edge of the road, but we didn't want to be left behind. I decided we would walk backward, as we fired our weapons in the direction of the machine gun. I kept the BAR firing, and the machine gun didn't answer our fire. We made it around the curve to safety. We were lucky.

We rejoined the platoon, and took cover in a small inn on the northeast side of the Halte intersection about 60 yards from the road. We no sooner had settled in than heavy mortar shells started landing on the building. The second floor was getting clobbered. We retreated to the basement. We could see the buildings at the intersection from the cellar windows in front of the inn. The mortar barrage stopped, and a Mark III tank came down the road from where we had just been.

When the German tank commander had almost reached the two-story building at the intersection, he closed his hatch, moved up to the building and stopped. At a right angle to the German tank, around the corner of the two-story building, was an American Sherman tank. The two tanks were out of sight of each other. The ends of their cannons almost touched. The tank commanders were hidden from each other by the corner of the building even though they were only a few feet apart. In just a minute or two, the German tank backed up the road it had just come down. As we watched from our cellar window, I wondered if we should fire a bazooka round at the tank. We didn't because we didn't want to draw his fire, and the tank made good its retreat. Very shortly after the tank was out of sight, an American ambulance came tearing down the road from Les Xatis, went around the Sherman tank, and turned left up the road the German tank had just left on. We didn't hear any firing, but the ambulance didn't return, and I am sure it was captured. Then I felt sorry we didn't fire at the tank. I wouldn't have questioned our caution if the ambulance hadn't wandered in on the scene.

Fifty years later, I attended a reunion of the 3rd Medical Battalion and met the man riding in the right seat of that ambulance. They were looking for one of the division's cub airplanes that had been shot down near the German main line of resistance. They found the plane, but were soon captured by German infantry. They spent the war in a POW (Prisoner of War) camp working in the camp infirmary with a German doctor who treated them well. I was glad to learn the tank had not fired at them!

We stayed in that position for a few more hours, and then we moved up on the hill area named Boir des Rapailles de Bemont. It was a dense, forested hill. I remember sending out a food and ammo detail that night. I am sure the Germans were very close by on the hill, but our platoon had no fire fights, attacks, or counter attacks. Other units of the 15th Infantry were heavily engaged with the enemy in this area, and on this same hill above the rock quarry. We moved once or twice to new positions during the next few days, and then were pulled off the hill on October 3rd.

The next morning "I" Company was ordered to attack back in the same area we first ran into the farmhouse and the Germans. We moved up the same road, past the curve, and past the burned out farmhouse. It was early in the morning, dark and foggy. You could only see ten feet or so. We were deployed in a skirmish line on the edge of an open field on the knoll above the house. The ground had been recently plowed. We moved out in a cautious and very quiet manner. It was a gentle climb in the plowed field, and we were nearly blind in the fog. No one explained what we were expected to do or find. After about 10 to 15 minutes of slow steady advancement, we came to the edge of a forest. There was the slightest bit of twilight now. Suddenly right in front of me, not more than four feet away, was a German soldier sitting on a stump. He had a sniper's rifle in his left hand, the rifle butt was on the ground. A short leather cover was over the muzzle. Our eyes met. We saw each other at the same moment! He didn't make a move. I covered him with my M-1 rifle, and he surrendered to me. I later learned the Germans had dug a fairly deep hole, about 6 by 6 by 5 feet, in the middle of the field we had just crossed. They had suspended a truck tire rim on a tripod, and they had an iron bar in the dugout to sound the alarm if the Americans approached. Fortunately, because of the plowed ground, and the foggy, dark morning, the two Germans on duty at the alarm were captured before they realized what was happening. That was the only time we saw such an alarm, and I don't understand why they built that warning system. A machine gun may have been in the dugout, and would have been of more value. Its sound would have alerted the Germans just as well.

I had no sooner captured the German soldier than we were under heavy fire from just inside the forest. We took cover at the edge of the small forest, and engaged the Germans in a heavy firefight that lasted the better part of the day. We finally pushed through to the other edge of the forest and saw, less than 50 yards away, the Cleurie Quarry. Following heavy mortar barrages and direct tank fire, we moved over a large pile of rock, and onto the northwest rim of the quarry. Units of the lst and 3rd Battalions were in on this final assault. As we made our final attack, the surviving Germans pulled out to the north. Only a few Germans were captured after the long day of fighting. Audie Murphy, who ended the war as the most decorated soldier in World War II, led his B Company platoon on this attack. I commanded a platoon from "I" Company. We were both Staff Sergeants at the time. Our six-day battle for the quarry was the worst fighting for "I" Company since Anzio. It was the first of many battles to follow, as we pushed through the Vosges Mountains.

October and November, 1944 in the cold, rainy forest of the Vosges, were trying and very dangerous times. Could we penetrate the Vosges Mountains, cross the Meurthe River, and capture Strasbourg? Yes, we did it, but there were many roadblocks ahead.

Defeated and dejected enemy file out of the Cleurie quarry after its reduction by 3rd Division troops.

8. Road block

"Impassable?" So it seemed. The only paths for advancement through our area of the Vosges Mountains were narrow, easily defended, winding roads that cut through heavily forested mountains and valleys. The Germans made the most of the terrain in developing their defenses.

Our division was a spearhead division for the 7th U.S. Army. We had many difficult battles in the Vosges in October and November of the fateful year the Allies drove the Germans out of France. The clouds hung low in the Vosges, and it was frequently raining and cold. It was the worst weather in 25 years. Firewood was everywhere, but fires were rarely allowed. Smoke draws artillery fire, and almost anything is preferable to an artillery barrage.

Certain battles are vividly imprinted in any fighting man's memory. A battle for a roadblock near St. Die is one I remember well. We were advancing east on a narrow mountain road. "I" Company was on the point for the 3rd Battalion of the 15th Infantry Regiment. My platoon was leading "I" Company. As Platoon Sergeant, I was with the lead squad. The Squad's two scouts were about 75 yards in front of us. Scouts are terribly vulnerable. They must lead the advance as point men, probing for the enemy, usually in the open, as they were this day. They are often fired upon before they see the enemy. It was about two in the afternoon on a gray October day. Our two scouts drew enemy fire as they rounded a curve in the road. I really don't know what happened to them as they drew a fusillade of small arms fire that started our battle for the roadblock.

Fortunately, the platoon was back far enough to be protected, and that is the reason for scouts out well ahead of the main body. We took cover in the ditches alongside the road. My platoon had just received a replacement Platoon Leader. 1st Lieutenant Robinson arrived the night before while we were occupying a house several miles back from the roadblock. It was dark when he joined us. He was probably pretty nervous, and a half an hour after he arrived, a shot rang out in the dark room where we were resting. The Lieutenant's carbine discharged while he was cleaning it. No one was injured, but in a room crowded with combat weary G.I.'s, it was hardly a propitious start for a new Platoon Leader. Lt. Robinson, at the rear of the platoon, was soon joined by "I" Company Commander, Captain Stuart. They decided to bring up a Sherman tank to probe the roadblock. The tank was temporarily assigned to our company from the division's tank battalion. Tank crews hated such assignments, but in the infantry that is one way the tanks were used. A soldier with a mine detector led the tank up alongside our platoon. The soldier moved aside, and the tank cautiously rounded the curve, and drew fire from an anti-tank gun, or a self-propelled gun. Fortunately the shell missed, and the tank withdrew to safety.

Captain Stuart ordered our platoon to make a flanking attack up a hill through the forest on the right side of the road. Lt. Robinson was at the lead of one squad, and I was in the lead of another. The men of the two squads were deployed in a skirmish line to our left and right rear. The Lieutenant and I were on the point of a wedge as we moved up the hill. In combat it is hard to get men to advance into certain gunfire. Platoon Leaders and Platoon Sergeants often take the lead, even though it is not where they should be on such attacks.

We advanced very carefully from tree to tree, stump to rock. We moved steadily. We hadn't seen the enemy, and they hadn't fired on us. It was a moderately steep hill, and my eyes constantly scanned the terrain in front looking for the enemy I knew was there. Then I saw what I was looking for. Near the crest of the hill about 60 yards away, and through a fairly open area, I saw two dreaded German helmets side by side behind a log. Under the front brim of each helmet were two dark shadows hiding eyes I knew were watching us. The moment I saw the helmets, I shouted, "down!", and all hell broke loose. Machine guns and rifles sprayed a deadly hail of bullets all about us from the Germans who had been lying in wait for us.

In a forest there is a lot of cover, and we made the most of it. Lt. Robinson was on my left behind a tree. I was behind a boulder. The men took cover down the hill behind us. The Lieutenant had orders to advance our platoon up the hill, and he waved me forward. I told him there was no way we could move up that hill. The men behind us were not in a position to set down a base of fire over the Germans. Although Lt. Robinson was inexperienced, he was conscientious, and he felt compelled to follow orders. He kept waving me forward. I looked back at the squad, and caught the eyes of one or two men. I motioned them to move forward. I picked out a tree about 10 feet to my front, and sprinted to new cover drawing a burst of gunfire. As I looked back, no one followed. Fortunately I wasn't hit. Lt. Robinson then realized we couldn't go forward, and he signaled us to withdraw. We worked our way down the hill without a single casualty.

By the time we arrived at a gully at the foot of the hill a 60mm mortar crew from the 4th Platoon had set up, and was ready to fire. There was only a small opening in the canopy of the dense forest to fire shells through. It was tricky, but the mortar crew was experienced. Even so, the first shell left the tube and struck a branch overhead. Shell fragments fell about us without causing an injury. Nothing was harmed except pride. A quick-witted mortarman yelled "counter battery", a feeble attempt at humor.

Lt. Robinson suggested the tank be pulled off the road, and it headed up the hill with my platoon following close behind. I didn't think the tank would be able to climb out of the gully, but it did, and we had to leave the safety of the ditch, and start up the hill again. This time we headed back up the hill in several bunched-up ragged lines crowded behind the tank for cover.

The tank cannon fire and machine guns kept the Germans off balance and seeking cover, and the tank gave us cover to the front as we moved forward. We advanced up the hill until enemy fire from our flanks forced us to leave the tank and take cover behind boulders and trees. All forward movement stopped.

After considerable delay, preparations were made to fire heavy mortars on the forward German positions. While we waited, I remember our Regimental Commander, Lt. Col. Edson, was standing behind a tree talking to our Company Commander, Capt. Stuart. Edson, a West Pointer, clean shaven and dressed in neat O.D.'s, made a striking contrast with Stuart, who looked like a character out of a Bill Mauldin cartoon. Edson was a fine commander, and was anxious to get Stuart and "I" Company's attack moving. While they were talking, a German artillery shell whined overhead and crashed nearby. G.I.'s almost always take cover at the sound of an incoming shell, and Stuart hit the dirt. Col. Edson stood cool and erect behind the tree. I was nearby, and remember the Colonel telling Stuart that perhaps his "excessive" caution was the reason the attack was stalled. I thought the Colonel was unfair, but Capt. Stuart was very cautious, a trait that bothered the Colonel a lot more than it bothered us. Often caution is the better part of valor!

After a heavy mortar and artillery barrage, we moved forward. The Germans retreated to a new position 60 or 70 yards behind their original line. We took several casualties on this attack. One rifleman was killed firing his rifle from behind the same tree I was using. He was standing, and I was near the ground. I felt a little guilty, because I had the safest position. It was getting dark fast, and we were ordered to dig in. The Germans were only 30 to 40 yards away. It soon grew very dark, and impossible to see even a few feet away.

Earlier that day we had traded our C rations with the tankers for a ten-in-one "crew" ration. Their ration came in two boxes, and as we moved forward, two men each carried a box. It was a very foolish trade, and the only time I ever remember doing that. We ate C rations day after day for months, and wanted something different, although preparing the "crew" ration would have been difficult for us. I don't think any of us had ever seen the inside of such a ration box. A man who was killed that evening carried one of the boxes. I knew where he had fallen, and it wasn't far from where we were digging in. It wasn't completely dark, so I ventured forward through the forest about 25 feet toward where I thought the ration box was. I soon heard German voices very near by and decided it was better to go hungry than take any more chances.

We dug our foxholes in fairly soft ground, two men to a hole as usual. G.I.'s like to cover the holes with branches, twigs, and dirt to protect themselves from shell fragments. Tree bursts are especially dangerous in a forest. Finding cover for the holes was nearly impossible because of the darkness and the close proximity of the Germans. Two enterprising soldiers did make a cover for their foxhole. The next morning, we looked in amazement at their creation. They had found a pile of Panzerfausts, a German anti-tank weapon something like our bazooka. Our platoon had never before seen this German anti-tank weapon up close enough to handle. It was a high explosive warhead on one end of a two-inch diameter tube, about four feet long, filled with a rocket propellant. Two soldiers, who had found a pile of these strange weapons near their foxhole, neatly laid the Panzerfausts across the top of their foxhole alternating ends of the warheads so the tubes could be close together. They covered this deadly arrangement with twigs and dirt, thinking they had improved their chances of surviving an artillery barrage. Fortunately, their cover was never tested.

Every foxhole on our perimeter had one person awake and alert with rifle and hand grenades ready for the slightest sound to our front. It was always hard for me to stay awake for a whole hour, so my foxhole mate and I alternated, sometimes on the half hour. G.I.'s in combat are always tired from long marches, fighting, patrolling, ration and ammo details, digging and manning foxholes, etc. Sleep is the most wonderful thing in the world. You never get enough, and staying awake can be very difficult, at least, it was for me. That night was very scary, and no doubt, everyone on guard was awake and alert.

The next morning mortar and tank fire softened the Germans, and we moved over the crest of the hill into their positions.

In a well-constructed German dugout I found part of a loaf of dark bread and several cans of German rations. The can I opened contained lima beans and pieces of ham. It was the best meal I had in months. It tasted much better than our C rations, and I was hungry from missing my meal the night before. About four feet in front of me was a German soldier with a terrible head wound lying face down in the dirt with the top of his head facing me. Part of his skull bone was gone, and a portion of his brain was exposed. At my left, about three feet away, was another German soldier stretched out face down. A light machine gun was alongside his left arm. I took them both for dead.

I was sitting on the edge of the dugout eating the delicious bread and beans when, suddenly, the German soldier in front of me moved his head, and tried to raise up a little way on one elbow. Half of his face, and part of his skull, was gone. It didn't seem possible that he was alive. He uttered a very faint sound and collapsed. I had killed my share of enemy soldiers, but I had never killed a prisoner or a wounded man. If ever a mercy killing was justified, I was sure this was one, but I hesitated; it seemed wrong, yet it seemed merciful, and I ended the poor man's life. When I fired my rifle, the "dead" soldier on my left came to his knees, thrust his hands into the air, and in a fearful, trembling voice begged me not to shoot.

This was my first experience with a German feigning death. I was so surprised I momentarily froze. Two men from my platoon moved towards him, kicked the machine gun aside, and grabbed his wristwatch. After weapons, a watch was the first thing a G. I. looks for. I kicked myself for moving so slow, while my G.I. comrade added another watch to his collection of four or five already on his arm.

The battle for the roadblock was typical of many in the Vosges, yet many unique experiences had occurred. It was the first time I had ever seen a mortar shell explode over the head of its crew. You rarely see a Regimental Commander on the very front lines. It was the only time I remember trading C rations for a "crew" ration. It was the first time our platoon had handled Panzerfausts, and was probably the only time in the war they were used to cover a foxhole. It was the first and only time I ever thought a killing was justified in mercy, and a second later, the only time I ever encountered a German soldier playing dead just a few feet from me. It had been a difficult battle, and I was glad to hear the command, "fall in", back on the road we had been driven off the day before. As we moved off the hill and down to the road, what I remember most was the pitiful cries of wounded Germans scattered among the shell holes and broken trees on a terribly scarred hillside. I worried that our medics might not find some of them.

Our advance on the formidable Vosges had been held up for 18 hours with many dead and wounded on both sides. The German commanders were probably happy with an 18-hour delay. Our commanders were happy we were moving again. It was a terrible price to pay for such a small part of France, but in North Africa, Sicily, Italy, France, Germany, and Austria, 25,000 men of the Third Infantry Division were killed or wounded in similar battles.

Infantry was one of the worst kinds of duty, yet it required the utmost sense of purpose, endurance, courage, and sacrifice. The survivors of such battles are lucky, but even after a lucky survival it is their lot to face the next battle. It was no wonder G.I.'s welcomed certain types of wounds and illness. It was their only legitimate escape. While most infantrymen would rather not return to the front, if they have to go back into combat when their wounds are healed or their illness cured, they want to rejoin their original units. You want to be with your friends, and you want to be in an outfit you know. In the Third Division you knew you were in one of the best outfits in the U.S. Army.

Risking one's life in combat requires a strong devotion to one's country and to the men in your unit. We had that devotion. The war to defeat the Axis was just. There was no alternative. The roadblock had to be taken.

9. A long night

In late October, 1944, the 3rd Battalion, 15th Inf. Regt. was dug in on the southwest bank of the Meurthe River near St. Die, France. Plans were being made for a river crossing by elements of the 3rd Infantry Division. Every night we could hear the Germans preparing defensive positions about 150 yards north of the river. We could hear pounding, clanking, and the movement of vehicles.

One night orders came to "I" Company to provide a reconnaissance patrol for the Battalion S-2. The 3rd Platoon Leader, myself, the Platoon Sergeant, and six men were detailed for the patrol. We were to find a ford, cross the river, move up to the enemy's position, capture a prisoner, and bring back as much information as possible about the enemy's position and activities.

It was after dark, about 8 p.m., when we moved down to the river's bank. Several of the taller men were lowered into the river to find footing where we could cross. Communication wire was tied around their waist for safety. They couldn't find a place where they could get across the river. The river was deep and swift.

We pulled back a short distance and waited. We had only made a feeble effort to find a ford. The lieutenant decided to report back to the S-2 (battalion intelligence officer) that we couldn't find a way across the river afoot. The patrol waited outside the Battalion Headquarters while Lt.____ made his report. The S-2 wasn't satisfied. We were sent back to the river. This time we didn't even try to attempt a ford. Several men were asked to get wet, so it appeared we tried. After awhile, back to headquarters we went. The lieutenant made a report while we waited. The S-2, I am sure, could sense Lt.____ was lying. In any event, we were sent back to the river again, but this time we carried an inflatable six-man rubber raft. We stopped at the river's edge, and made no attempt to cross.

About midnight, Lt. _____ reported to the S-2 we couldn't cross, or something to that effect. Fortunately, only the lieutenant had to face the S-2. Again, we were ordered to try to cross. We were all guilty of conspiring to avoid danger. I felt very uncomfortable about being part of a lie. Since it was late, and everyone was tired, and some of the men were wet and cold, I told Lt.____ it wasn't right to ask the men to go down again after what we had put them through. I suggested we send the men back to their dugouts, and that he and I try to cross the river. He concurred. The two of us went back to the river. We were both over six feet tall. I tied the wire around my waist, and entered the swift moving water. I kept feeling for footing and eventually made it across. The water was up to my neck in places. I carried my rifle overhead. The rain-swollen river was a good 60 feet wide where we crossed. After I was on the north bank, Lt._____ followed, and I gathered in the wire as he crossed. We found ourselves in thick rushes or tulles in a sort of marshland. We cautiously moved towards the German lines for about 100 yards. The sound of enemy construction grew very loud. We paused and considered our next move. It was about 3 a.m. We decided the faint light and the possibility of mines made further movement risky. We beat a retreat across the river without trying for a prisoner.

We crossed safely, and made it back to the S-2 about 4 a.m.. This time I was invited inside the S-2's house. I waited in a small foyer while Lt.____ made his report. In a short while I was asked to make a report. I could only tell the truth about our last effort. I don't remember being asked about our first three "attempts". The S-2, a captain, was a small, feisty, tough, competent, intelligence officer. I could sense the S-2 was disgusted and angry. We were dismissed, and made it back to our dug outs about 4:30 am. It had been a long night.

The next morning I was summoned to Battalion Headquarters. I was informed Lt._____ was under arrest, and would stand court martial for lying and dereliction of duty. I was told, as second in command of the patrol, I was also responsible for what happened the night before. A river crossing had to be made under fire, and lives depended on accurate intelligence. I felt terrible I had let my outfit down. I had a good record, but there was no excuse. I expected the worse.

Unknown to me, I had been put in for a battlefield commission. I was informed of this, but was now told that such a commission was out of the question. We had been in constant combat for two and a half months. It was decided, in view of my good record, I needed a rest. Another platoon sergeant and I were the first men from "I" Company to be given leave to Paris. We spent five glorious days in the newly liberated French capital. I couldn't have been more surprised, or pleased, with my "sentence". When we returned to the company, the Meurthe River had been crossed. Lt._____, while under arrest in the platoon headquarters' house, had been hit by shell fragments from German artillery. When he was evacuated, he wasn't expected to live.

Once again I was Acting Platoon Leader. Not being commissioned didn't bother me a bit. Platoon Sergeants seem to live longer than Platoon Leaders.

There is good and bad in all of us. It took me a long time before I told anyone of my conduct on the Meurthe River. Self-preservation is a strong motive, but in combat it must be balanced against one's duty. I made a mistake that night. It didn't happen again.

10. Attack — Counterattack

In Southern Italy, and on the Anzio Beachhead, the GIs of the 3rd Infantry Division would wishfully think, "Rome and Home". It wasn't to be.

After the capture of Rome, the Third Division spearheaded the Southern France Invasion. After 110 days of continuous fighting from the French Riviera to Strasbourg on the Rhine, the GI's thoughts might have been, "The Rhine and Rest". I never heard the expression.

No division deserved rest more. The soldiers that survived the beachhead landings, the many fire fights and skirmishes, the long forced marches up the Rhone Valley, the stubborn resistance in the Vosges Mountains, the Merthe River crossing, and the final push through Alsace-Lorraine to Strasbourg, badly needed rest and relaxation. The fight to capture Strasbourg in late November was the first of three times the Third Division would fight to the Rhine River. The Third Infantry Division was either the first or second American division to reach the Rhine River.

Strasbourg is a large, beautiful city, and we were glad we were alive, and in possession of this ancient Roman outpost. Our field kitchens rolled into company bivouacs, and hot meals were served by company cooks for only the second time since landing in France.

Issues of clean O.D's replaced filthy, ragged uniforms that contained months of grime and filth. Replacements filled our ranks, and my platoon was full strength for the first time since we hit the beach at St. Tropez. During the two weeks we were in Strasbourg, our company's rifle platoons took turns manning old pill boxes of the Maginot Line facing the Germans across the Rhine.

When not on outpost, we were training. I never did get to see any of the interesting sights in Strasbourg. I was detailed to a three-day artillery school for platoon sergeants with the 39th Field Artillery. We spent one day with the 105 howitzers that supported the 15th Infantry Regiment, one day at fire control, the command post that made sure artillery shells didn't hit our troops, and did hit the Germans, and one day as a forward observer. The time I spent in a third story factory window directing artillery fire was my first look at German soil.

Christmas was only a week away, and company cooks were laying in supplies for a real Christmas dinner. After three days of fighting in Strasbourg, it was quiet in the Strasbourg sector. Although we didn't know it (at least in the ranks), the Battle of the Bulge had started several hundred miles to our north. The German Army was making considerable progress along the front facing the U.S. First and Ninth Armies.

South of Strasbourg the German Army, with many fighting SS units, was holding the last French soil the Germans occupied in all of France. It was the wine district of Alsace-Lorraine, and the German salient was to be known as the "Colmar Pocket". Hitler had high hopes of breaking out of the Colmar Pocket, recapturing Strasbourg, and exploiting the gains made against the Americans in their Ardennes offensive.

Heinrich Himmler, chief of the SS, was in command in Colmar making sure the Germans held onto their valuable Rhine bridgehead.

Our "rest and relaxation" came to an abrupt end on December 19th. In less than an hour we struck camp, and climbed aboard trucks heading south. We didn't know much about the "big picture", but we did know disappointment leaving our kitchen truck and hot meals, and the possibility of a real Christmas dinner.

It was a cold, rainy day as we headed south under the canvas covers of the trucks. We didn't pay any attention to the countryside we traveled through, but soon enough we disembarked and started marching in the rain. The Third Division was relieving the 36th Infantry Division. They had been engaged in furious battles with the Germans for several weeks, and they were in bad shape. My company was in battalion reserve. Third Battalion Headquarters was in a large house and winery in the middle of a vineyard about a mile from the German positions. We found shelter in several of the nearby buildings. My platoon spent two nights in a barn. Since we were about a mile behind the front, we were relatively safe, as we bedded down by the rock wall foundation. I remember sitting in a small group near the wall sharing a box of cookies that had just arrived from my home. The cookies had to be over a month old, and they were delicious. December 22 passed, and we didn't have the slightest idea of what was happening. We were glad we were in reserve, but our good fortune didn't last another day. The next morning "I" Company was ordered to capture Bennwihr, a small town that, along with Mittelwihr and Sigolsheim, all in German hands, created an undesirable bulge in the American lines.

As morning darkness lightened on December 23, we formed the company, and marched to the edge of a vineyard, our "line of departure" for the attack.

Four Sherman medium tanks arrived to take part in the attack. They were tanks from the Division's Tank Battalion. We had to attack through a vineyard. The tanks would lead the way, knocking down vines and wire, so we could follow in the tank tracks. It would be safer walking in the tank tracks if the Germans had planted any anti-personal mines.

My platoon, the Third, would have two tanks leading it, and the First Platoon on our left would follow two tanks. The Second Platoon would follow in reserve. The four tanks would move abreast of each other. My platoon leader, First Lieutenant William Courtney, was behind one tank leading a squad, and I was behind the other tank with a squad. Our reserve squad brought up the rear behind my squad. It was just turning daylight when we moved out. We made good progress through the vineyard, and went about a half-mile before engaging the enemy.

As we approached the German positions, mortar and artillery shells started coming in. The shells exploded about us, but we kept moving with the tanks, as it was the best way to get through the barrage. Suddenly, I felt a terrific pain behind my right knee. I had been hit by a shell fragment. My O.D. pants and winter long-johns had been torn. I reached through the torn clothing, and felt my leg. I could feel the area where it hurt, but I couldn't find any blood or torn flesh. I reached into the torn clothing again in a desperate search for my "wound", and felt for blood. My hand came out again without blood. There was torn clothing, even through skin clinging long-johns, a severe burning sensation, pain, but no wound.

It was a great disappointment. I had fought on the Anzio-Nettuno Beachhead on the breakout to capture Rome, on the invasion at St. Tropez, I had fought four months in France to reach this unknown vineyard. A wound was an infantryman's legitimate escape from battle. A light leg wound could save your life. It was one of the better things that could happen to an infantryman. I soon realized my "million dollar wound" was not a reality. My examination caused me to fall back a little, and as I caught up with the platoon, all hell broke loose,

The tanks moved ahead of us, and were engaged in heavy firing. Almost instantly all four tanks were hit and abandoned. The tank crews streamed out of the hatches, and several of the tanks started to burn. We moved around the tanks in a skirmish line with all of our weapons firing at German dugouts. We overran the German position on the edge of the town. My Platoon Leader was badly wounded, but we supported him, as we moved into the town. We found shelter in the basement of a completely destroyed house in the center of a courtyard just off the main street. Bennwihr had been destroyed by fierce fighting between the 36th Division and the Germans. There was little left but piles of rubble, and badly damaged buildings. Only three pre-war houses exist in Bennwihr. The lieutenant and several other wounded men were cared for in the cellar. I posted what men were left along the wall of the courtyard, and a few were left to guard the cellar.

I am not sure what our objective was that morning, but we had penetrated the German main line of resistance, and occupied a courtyard on the far side of the main road. We were in no condition to press the attack further. The rear wall of the courtyard was broken in places by artillery fire. I positioned myself near the wall that formed the back of a farm implement shed. The roof was blown away except for a few rafters. I peeked over a broken portion of the wall. In front of me 30 feet away were about 15 German soldiers gathered about an officer or non-com. Right below me about eight feet away against the wall was a German soldier peeking around the corner of the wall where it met the street. I pulled my head back, and grabbed a hand grenade from the holder on my belt. I pulled the pin and threw the grenade over the wall in the direction of the Germans. In my haste, I wasn't careful, and the hand grenade hit the rafter above me. Luckily, the momentum carried it over the wall, but just barely. It exploded far from its target. I moved down the wall and looked over; the Germans had scattered without injury. About that time, an explosion occurred in the rafter near me. I think it was a hand grenade. I was not injured.

I tried to contact my Company Commander on the walkie-talkie. I couldn't make contact. I decided to send the platoon runner back with a message about our condition and location, and report we were nearly surrounded and under counter attack. He left the courtyard at the opening into the main street. As he moved onto the street, the machine gunner on an unseen Mark IV tank tried to cut him down and nearly succeeded. The runner had lost his rifle and helmet, and returned to me, breathless, with news of the tank just down the road. I tried again to reach the company commander, and this time made radio contact. I told him we were surrounded on three sides by Germans and that a Mark IV was very near by. I thought the best thing to do was bring down artillery on the tank and the surrounding area. We would take cover the best we could. I gave him the coordinates of our position from my map, and soon 105mm shells from our artillery were falling close by, as we took cover in the cellar. The walls of the cellar extended about two feet above ground, and had windows on three sides with the cellar opening at the fourth side. We took up firing positions at the cellar windows and the cellar entrance.

While we had been at the walls of the courtyard, unknown to me, six Germans had rushed the cellar entrance through the courtyard entrance. Two of the Germans had been killed and were lying dead in the courtyard, two others had been wounded and captured, and two broke off the attack and retreated to safety. The two wounded Germans had joined our wounded in the cellar. They were given cigarettes, and their wounds were bound.

About the time we left the walls and took cover from the artillery, the Mark IV tank started to move on the street in front of the courtyard. The tank moved into sight at the courtyard entrance. He stopped momentarily, as if contemplating a turn into the courtyard. After a moment, he moved forward without trying to turn his cannon towards us. It was a great relief to hear him move down the street away from the entrance. Our relief was very fleeting. Almost as quickly as he had started forward, he reversed course. He backed up to the entrance and stopped. The tank cannon started to traverse to the right. The tank attempted a tight right turn, and the cannon moved some more. After several back and forth movements, the tank and its cannon were facing us, and moving toward the cellar opening. It was less than 60 feet away. As it was turning, I fired three rifle grenades at the tank without stopping it. We didn't have a Bazooka. The tank started firing at the cellar, as we hugged the walls for cover. Several 75mm shells crashed into the building. Shell fragments, pieces of the building, and clouds of dust engulfed us. After several shells exploded, something hit me on the right side of my face. I was momentarily stunned, and then numb with the realization I had been hit. My lips and right cheek were lacerated, and most of the teeth on the right side of my face were shattered. I was bleeding from the mouth as I moved deeper into the cellar. I had already thrown away the treasured German Luger pistol I kept in a shoulder holster. It wasn't smart to be captured with enemy equipment on your person. Everyone in the cellar realized we would soon be overrun. We knew German riflemen would be right behind the tank. Soon grenades and bullets from machine guns would find us if we didn't give up. We had our two German prisoners yell as loud as they could not to fire. We surrendered. We really had no alternative. Immediately German soldiers were ordering us out of the cellar.

There were 11 of us in the cellar, six were wounded. The lieutenant was still alive, but in very bad shape. The able bodied helped the wounded, as we made our way up into courtyard. I didn't need assistance and could move without help. I was the only wounded person standing alone and unaided.

They made a quick check for weapons and ordered us to move out of the courtyard. A German soldier led the way followed by the 11 of us. I was in the rear of the column followed by a German corporal.

As I was leaving the cellar, I looked about to see if I could find a place to hide. I had my long-desired wound, but I didn't want to be a prisoner, or be treated in German hospitals. As the Germans marched us back through a "no-man's land" on the main street I kept falling back until there was about 15 feet between me and the next American soldier. An occasional artillery shell would explode nearby. The German corporal realized it was no place to be moving slowly. He moved up next to my left side and gave me a slight push on my left shoulder saying, "mach schnell" (move quickly). He was a short man, about 5'6". He hadn't shaved for about three days, and the red stubble whiskers were prominent on his rather kind face. He carried an American M1 carbine in his left hand. My arms were in the air with my hands about level with my ears. As he touched my left shoulder, I turned to my left, and crashed the palm of my right hand into his chin. I can still see and feel the red whiskers. I wheeled to my right, and bolted into the rubble. I never saw the corporal fall, but I know my blow must have knocked him out. No rifle shots cracked near me, as I moved through the rubble toward the American lines. I moved rapidly through the broken buildings until I came to the next road running parallel to the main street. I turned right and moved along the edge of the road hugging the buildings. I soon saw American soldiers in the windows and doorways of several buildings. They were men from "I" Company's Second Platoon. They couldn't imagine how I could walk up that road without drawing fire. They had been shooting at Germans all morning in a winery and several other buildings that bordered the road.

I was directed to the company commander's command post. When I arrived at his cellar command post, I realized why I couldn't make consistent radio contact. When he was in the cellar, our radios would not function because they were not in a direct line.

I reported we had been in the courtyard, but now all of my platoon I knew about were either killed, wounded, or captured. I was the only one who escaped capture. I realized later some members of the platoon, mostly members of the reserve squad, had not made it to the courtyard and were okay.

I was taken to the Battalion aid station, and was given morphine and fluids. An ambulance ride took me to the 51st Evacuation Hospital in St. Die. My million-dollar leg wound eluded me, but my million-dollar face wound was almost as good. I would miss two and a half months of bitter winter fighting. While I was under treatment at the First General Hospital in Paris, and at a general hospital near Liverpool, England, the Third Division, fighting with the First French Army, captured Colmar in February, 1945, and made good its second approach to the Rhine River.

In March, 1945 the Division fought through the Siegfried Line near Zweibrucken, and approached the Rhine River for the third time. There were three weeks of difficult fighting in this sector. The Division crossed the Rhine at Worms after moderate fighting for the bridgehead.

In late March, I rejoined my Regiment for the final battles in Southern Germany. Our last and biggest battle in Germany was for Nuremberg. After five difficult days, Nuremberg fell. All of us felt the war was over, and that we would survive with any luck at all.

I often think about my comrades that were captured with me at Bennwihr, December 23, 1944. I know Lieutenant Courtney died in captivity. I don't know the fate of the rest, but I hope they made it home.

Abandoned German Mark IV Tank in Bennwihr, France –
December, 1944

Bennwihr, France, December, 1944.

Dünamünde, around December 1914

11. Prisoners

The Third Infantry Division participated in its tenth and last campaign in Europe as it swept through Southern Germany in the final phase of World War II. The majority of the fighting was small fire fights and skirmishes often at hastily erected roadblocks on the outskirts of villages and towns. The few German soldiers, often old men or young teenagers, manning these crude fortifications had no heart for our overwhelming strength in tanks, artillery, and men. Most of these positions fell with only the slightest resistance.

The Division did have some major battles in its last campaign, and the last was the capture of Nuremberg. The Germans had assembled artillery, anti-aircraft 88's, infantry, and tanks, for a determined stand in this important German city, the home and symbol of Nazism. A few armed German civilians joined in the battle. The Third Division fought five difficult days before the city surrendered. We knew, or at least hoped, this would be the last real battle of the war in Germany; we did not want to get killed or maimed with the end so near!

There was considerable talk about a "German Redoubt", an area in the Bavarian and Austrian Alps where SS troops and fanatical Germans would fight to the end. Fortunately the Redoubt never materialized. When the 7th Infantry Regiment of our Division hoisted the American flag over Hitler's Eagle's Nest near Berchtesgaden, we were through fighting.

One of my memories of the last month of fighting through Germany, was the large number of German soldiers taken as prisoners. From March 15 to May 8, 1945 our Division captured 101,201 prisoners. In our other nine campaigns during 28 months of combat, we had taken only relatively few prisoners. Only 1500 prisoners were taken during four months of fighting on the Anzio-Nettuno Beachhead, and another 2000 were taken on the breakout of the Beachhead and the capture of Rome. In the campaign in the Vosges Mountains from Sept. 15 to January 1 (1944-45) about 7000 Germans were captured. Seeing tens of thousands of prisoners was a new experience for most of us. One day my Company Commander sent out two men to make contact with units of the 42 Infantry Division on our right. When our two men returned in about two hours, they were escorting 147 unarmed rear area German troops.

We became casual about taking prisoners, as the Germans wanted to surrender to the Western Allies.

They went to great effort to leave the Russian sector so they could be captured by American and British forces rather than the Russians. This casual attitude towards Germans wanting to surrender got me into trouble one early morning.

I commanded a platoon that was ordered to form a roadblock deep in a forest. At midnight we were instructed to leave our position, and rejoin our company at a small village on the outskirts of the city of Bamberg. At early dawn, after a long march, we exited the forest at the edge of a village. As we stood on the road looking through the gray mist into the village wondering about German resistance and planning our next move, a lone German soldier walked from the village towards us. He had no weapon or helmet, but was carrying six or seven canteens full of water. He moved towards me, as I beckoned him with, "kommen zee har" (come here).

We didn't share a common language, except for a few words, but with his eyes, the nod of his head, and hand gestures, he indicated I was to follow him. I anticipated a routine surrender of his unit. I took one rifleman with me, and the two of us followed the German down the road about 200 yards, and then moved up a gentle hill on a path through the forest. In about five minutes we came to a small clearing. As I stood at the edge of the clearing , I became apprehensive. What concerned me were about 40 German infantrymen sound asleep under great coats and blankets. Alongside them was a great variety of weapons, rifles, machine pistols, light machine guns, Panzerfausts, pistols, and hand grenades. Two American infantrymen were about to capture a fully equipped platoon of German infantrymen. I didn't expect trouble, but I did have to be careful. I left my compatriot at the entrance of the clearing, and moved about 40 feet to my left. We couldn't surround the body of men, but we could cover their perimeter pretty well. When we were in position, I had our German canteen bearer wake his comrades. These men were in a deep, deep sleep. In spite of our commands and shouting to wake, they hardly stirred. We wanted them to wake up, stand, put their hands in the air and move away from their weapons. Eventually there was some movement, and occasionally a man would get to his knees, straighten up, stretch, and yawn. Soon, a few were getting to their feet in a kind of sleepy daze. We continued to yell "hand in ho", our German version of "hands in the air".

I was standing next to a pine tree with a trunk about eight inches in diameter. After several minutes of trying to wake our captives, my trouble began. To my left rear I heard the click of a rifle bolt. I turned my head in the direction of the sound. Twenty-five feet away standing behind a fairly large tree was a German soldier. He had his rifle aimed at my head. I could only see his right eye, and a portion of his forehead, as he took cover behind his "large" tree. I did my best to hide behind my "little" tree. His rifle barrel looked like a cannon pointed at me; it was a tense moment! With one eye on his rifle, and glances at the main body of Germans, I soon saw what was happening. Just behind the German with the rifle, the forest floor dipped down a hill. I couldn't see anyone on the ground, but every 10 seconds or so, I would see a German soldier fleeing down the hill through the brush and trees. After about six men made their escape, the soldier with the rifle also ran away. I concluded a group of officers, or non-coms, were sleeping a short distance from the main body. There was no way I could stop them, as my first shot would have been my last. Any shooting would have been the end for me and my comrade.

My attention was now back on the main body. They slowly moved away from their weapons, dropping any pistols and grenades they were carrying. We finally grouped them at the edge of the clearing, but they were very nonchalant about the whole episode. I think I, and probably my companion, were the only ones that felt any fear or nervousness. We finally moved them down the hill, and rejoined our platoon. Soon we were back with our company. Two infantrymen had captured a well-armed platoon of Germans.

Even after 59 years, the sight of the gun barrel pointed at my head is a vivid memory. I can still feel the adrenaline rush when I hear the bolt click!

12. The end

A rifle company is not in constant contact with the enemy. Regiments and battalions and their companies are sometimes in reserve. Many times in an attack one company is back and two companies are forward in the attack. Sometimes attacks are single company attacks with other companies following behind to move through your position, or to flank the enemy position. Platoons often are in company reserve, and not in immediate contact with the enemy. Even squads of a platoon get a break from time to time in combat. One hears the sounds of battle to the front, and one worries about artillery and mortar attacks, but being out of rifle and machine gun fire, and not having to fire back is a real break for an infantryman.

After Rome was liberated we spent nearly two months training for the invasion of Southern France. I was out of the line for three months following a wound received Dec 23, 1944. There are many blank days in my memory of the war. I cannot remember certain battles some of my comrades remember well. When we gather at reunions, I will hear stories of different attacks that I cannot recall even though I was with the Company at the time.

There are anecdotes about my army life in the training areas, on leave, on travel, in the hospitals, etc. that I could write about, but I have only related combat stories I remember with some detail, because combat is an unique experience. No two people see a battle the same way. No two battles are the same. No one else could have written these stories. I hope you found them interesting, informative, and enjoyable.

Author near Frankenburg, Germany in command of L Company. 15th Infantry Regiment - October, 1945.

Author at the Abbey of Monte Cassino in January, 1993 with Father Agustino, 84, the only priest left at the Abbey who was there during the 1944 bombings.

*Author (on left) with Richard Guimond, L Co 15
th Infantry Regiment (on right). In the center is Jeff
Damby and his wife. Jeff's grandfather, a tank platoon
Commander, was killed a few miles from my "Fire Three
Tracers" story. This picture was taken at the 2003
Reunion of the Society of the Third Infantry Division in
St. Louis, Mo.*

110

APPENDICES

A: Autobiography

JOHN BURROUGHS SHIRLEY

Born: Dec. 8, 1924. Place: Santa Ana, California. Married: April 21, 1951 to Helen Freeman. Place: Berkeley, California.

I was born in Santa Ana, California, Dec. 8, 1924, and was raised on a small orange orchard in Costa Mesa, California. It was a wonderful place to grow up, and during the depression we always had something to eat, and wood to keep us warm. My father was a carpenter, but during the depression it was hard for him to get work. My mother was a registered nurse, and she could find work from time to time, usually as a private duty nurse. I milked a cow from about age ten until I graduated from high school. We had chickens, a large vegetable garden, fruit trees; we raised pigs, sheep, and veal for meat. I had lots of chores with the animals and the garden, helped with the dishes, and helped my mother hang clothes on long clothes lines. I was in 4-H and Future Farmers of America. I had a paper route from the seventh grade through high school. I wasn't involved in athletics, and had average grades in school until my last two years in high school when the grades improved.

After graduation from high school in 1942 I attended California Polytechnic College in San Luis Obispo studying to be a dairyman. I turned eighteen in 1942, was drafted three months later, did my basic training at Camp Cooke, CA, spent four months at Ft. Sill, OK, and then was posted overseas as an infantry replacement. I joined "I" Company, 15th Infantry Regiment., Third Infantry Division then fighting on the Anzio-Nettuno Beachhead. After the capture of Rome we made the invasion of Southern France, fought up the Rhone River Valley, crossed the Vosges Mountains, and captured Strasbourg. I was wounded Dec. 23, 1944 fighting in the Colmar Pocket, spent three months in hospitals in France and England, and then returned in late March, 1945 to the 15th Inf. for the final battles in Southern Germany. I was a Platoon Sgt. most of the war, and received a battlefield commission near the end of the war. Besides the Purple Heart, I was awarded the Silver Star and two Bronze Stars. I was in six campaigns and one invasion in the European Theater of Operations.

Following discharge from the Army I attended the University of California, Davis, and studied to be a veterinarian. I had good grades, and was accepted into the first veterinary class at Davis, graduating in 1952. I joined the Alpha Gamma Rho Fraternity, and was active in school affairs and intramural sports. Here I met Helen Freeman, and we were married in 1951. She was a home economics major at Davis. We have five grown children, Steven, James, Jean, Barbara, and Patricia; and we have four grandchildren, Danielle, Jesse, Lisa, and Jeffery; and six great-grandchildren.

Helen was a fine water color artist. She passed away in 2015 from Alzheimer's disease. She was a loving wife and mother.

I worked for a veterinarian in Ukiah for a year and a half, and then established my own practice in Livermore, CA in 1954. It was a large and small animal practice for nine years, and then it was limited to small companion animals. I have been active in community affairs, having served on the City Planning Commission, eight years on the City Council, two of the years as Mayor. I was also Chairman of the Alameda County Mayor's Conference. I have been active in my profession serving various offices of the California Veterinary Medical Association and the American Animal Hospital Association. I have also been active in variety of offices of the Society of the Third Infantry Division including National President.

I sold my practice in 1982, worked part time, and retired in 1987. I like golf, tennis, skiing, hiking and back packing, and continue to be active in Rotary and other community activities. I like to read non-fiction of all kinds, but mostly history and biographies. Helen and I liked to travel in the United States, and I have done some traveling in Africa, Asia, and Europe. I like Livermore, and plan to remain in my home for the foreseeable future. I exercise and watch my diet, and hope to live a long, healthy life. So far, so good!

Updated 2017

B: *Third Infantry Division*
"ROCK OF THE MARNE"

The 3rd Infantry Division (RA) was organized November, 1917 at Camp Greene, N. C. Cited for the Battle of the Marne for stopping the last major German offensive near Paris, the Division suffered 7000 battle causalities in three days on the Marne River. The Division participated in six campaigns in WW I, and sustained 16,856 battle casualties in a little over six months of combat.

The Division was one of only three regular army divisions prior to WWII. It was reorganized at Ft. Lewis, Washington in 1940 with units from Chingwangtao, China, and western U. S. Army Posts including the Presidio San Francisco. Historic units include the 7th Inf. Div. (Cottonbaler/Vancouver Barracks), the 15th Inf. Div. (Can Do/China), and the 30th Inf. Div. (Rock of the Marne/Presidio San Francisco): the 9th, 10th, 39th, and 41st Field Artillery Battalions. The WWII Commanding Generals were Jonathan W. Anderson, Wm A. Campbell, Lucian K. Truscott, Jr, John "Iron Mike" O'Daniel, and Robert N. Young. The higher commands were

Western Task Force and II U.S. Corp (Africa), U.S. 5th Army (Italy), U.S. 7th Army (Sicily, France, Germany, and Austria), and 1st French Army (Colmar Pocket).

In WWII, the 3rd Inf. Div. earned an astounding combat record unsurpassed by any other army division. Committed to action in "Operation Torch", the division landed at Fedala, French Morocco, Nov. 8,1942, and was attacking Casablanca when Vichy French forces asked for an armistice. The division was later moved to Tunisia to attack the enemy shortly before the Africa Corps surrendered. On July 10,1943, the Division landed in Sicily, and with hard fighting and long forced marches took Palermo in twelve days. A week later it struck out towards Messina, but its advance was halted when the Germans demolished a section of the highway from a cliff that dropped straight into the sea. Undaunted, the 10th Engineers replaced it with a bridge built on the side of the same cliff, a construction feat called a "bridge hung from the sky". The bridge was completed in 18 hours. German resistance was strong, and the 30th Inf. made two amphibious landings behind the German lines on this thrust . The Division entered Messina just before the arrival of British forces fighting from the south.

The 3rd Division was committed to the fight for Italy when it landed at Salerno on D+9. In difficult

116

terrain and terrible weather, the division fought its way north. Following the crossing of the Volturno, casualties were high from fighting in the mountains on the approach to Casino. Following the capture of Monte Rotundo, a key objective to neutralize Monte Lungo and Monte la Difensa, the division was taken from the line in December, 1943 to prepare for an amphibious landing behind the German lines at Anzio-Nettuno.

On January 22,1944, the 3rd Div. and the British 1st Inf. Division landed at Nettuno and Anzio to engage the enemy in the most bitter battles of WWII. In a series of attacks and counterattacks that costs many thousand of casualties on both sides of the front , the Germans stopped the Allies on the Beachhead, but could not annihilate them as ordered by Hitler. On May 23,1944, the Third Division led the attack off the Beachhead, that resulted in the capture of Cisterna, Highway 7, Cori, and the approaches to Artena and Highway 6 in several days of bitter fighting. On May 23, the division lost 995 men killed and wounded, the most casualties in WWII for a single division in one day. At Artena, the division took on an old adversary, the Herman Goring Panzer Division, as it attacked through Artena to cut Highway 6, and capture Valmontone. A few days later on June 4, 1944, the Division entered Rome, the First of the Axis capitals to fall. The honor of garrisoning Rome fell to the Third

Division, but the stay in Rome only lasted two weeks. The division moved to the Naples area to train for the Invasion of Southern France. On Aug 15, 1944 the division landed on beaches near San Tropez on the French Riviera. The German 19th Army withdrew from Southern France, but engaged U. S. forces in a brilliant series of rear guard actions, as the 3rd, 45th, and 36th Inf. Divisions fought north up the Rhone Valley. The 3rd Div. had four months of very costly and difficult battles fighting in the Vosges Mountains, culminating with the crossing of the Merthe River and the capture of Strasbourg in late November. The Battle of the Bulge started Dec 16, 1944 in the north, while south of Strasbourg, German forces fought desperately to hold the last of their French soil in the area of Colmar.

The Third Division was attached to the 1st French Army during the bloody battles to eliminate the "Colmar Pocket". On Feb 6, 1945, Neuf-Brisach fell to the Third Division, thus ending one of the Division's most costly and bitter campaigns. The entire division was awarded the Distinguished Unit Citation and a second French Fouraggere for the liberation of Colmar in the "best bit of maneuvering on the Western Front".

On March 13,1945, the 3rd Div. along with the 45th and the 100th Inf. Divs. spearheaded the drive through the Siegfried Line in the 7th Army sector. After a week of very hard fighting, the Siegfried line was breached on March 20th, and the Division crossed the Rhine south of Worms on March 26th. The division still faced last-ditch fanatical stands by German troops inside Germany en route to five days of difficult fighting for the capture of Nuremberg, home of Nazi socialism. Following the fall of Nuremberg, the division accepted the surrender of Augsburg, entered Munich after a few scattered fights, and raced to Salzburg, Austria. On May 5, 1945 men of the 7th Inf. Regt. of the 3rd Inf. Div. raised the American flag over Berchtesgaden, Hitler's mountain retreat in Austria. The war was over for the Third Division, and VE day was May 8th.

From Fedala, North Africa (Nov.,1942) till Berchtesgaden, Austria (May 1945), the Third Division participated in ten campaigns in the European Theater, fighting in Africa, the Mediterranean and Europe. The division sustained 24,878 battle casualties in 553 days of combat. Its troops earned 40 Medals of Honor (MOH), 172 Distinguished Service Crosses, over 4,817 Silver Stars, in excess of 6,000 Bronze Stars, 3 Distinguished Service Medals, 150 Legion of Merits, 98 Soldiers Medals, 115 Air Medals, 14 Distinguished Unit Citations, and 14 Meritorious Service Plaques. Over 26,000 Purples Hearts were awarded. Among the division's ranks was the legendary Lt. Audie L. Murphy (MOH), the most decorated soldier in US Army history. Another famous soldier of the division is Maurice "Footsie" Britt (MOH), the first U.S. soldier to earn our three highest awards for valor in one war.

The Division was called once again to battle in the Korean War. Following rapid deployment from Ft. Benning, GA under the able leadership of Maj. Gen. Robert Soule, the division was deployed in eastern North Korea in the Hamburg-Hungnam area. As the Allies were forced to retreat from the China Reservoir entrapment, the 3rd Div. fell back to the port of Hungnam. From Nov. 30 until Dec. 24, 1950 the 3rd Div. held the beachhead perimeter, often under heavy attack, and conducted the most massive beachhead evacuation in American military history: 105,000 troops, 100,000 refugees, 17,500 vehicles, and 750,000 tons of cargo. It was a masterful action that earned the Division and its commander fame and respect. The Division spent the next two years in battles fighting in eight Korean war campaigns. The Division earned 11 Medals of Honor, and suffered 10,391 battle casualties.

Since 1958, the Third Division (Mechanized) has been in the NATO Forces stationed in Würzburg, Germany.

It's Third Brigade (The Phantom Brigade) participated in the Gulf War, and other units of the Division had important assignments in support of Desert Storm.

In three major wars, the 3rd Inf. Div. earned 24 campaign streamers, more than 52,000 battle casualties, and has spent more than forty years overseas serving our Nation.

The 3rd Inf. Div. spearheaded the 2003 Iraq Invasion and was the first unit to enter Baghdad.

This history was prepared by Dave Lee, 7th Infantry Regiment, using information from *The History of the Third Division in WWII* and other publications.

C: The Dogface Soldier

This was a popular song that kept our spirits up

Moderato

I WOULD-N'T GIVE A BEAN TO BE A FAN-CY PANTS MAR-INE

—— I'D RA-THER BE A DOG-FACE SOL-DIER LIKE I

AM ——; I WOULD-N'T TRADE MY OLD—O D'S FOR

ALL THE NA-VY'S DUN-GA-REES FOR I'M THE WALK-ING

PRIDE OF UN-CLE SAM——; ON ALL THE POST-ERS THAT I

READ IT SAYS THE AR-MY BUILDS MEN—— SO THEY'RE

TEAR-ING ME DOWN TO BUILD ME O-VER A-GAIN—— I'M

JUST A DOG-FACE SOL-DIER WITH A RI-FLE ON MY

SHOUL-DER AND I EAT RED MEAT FOR BREAK-FAST EV'RY DAY

——, SO FEED ME AM—MUN-I-TION, KEEP ME

IN THE THIRD DIV-I-SION , YOUR DOG-FACE SOL-DIER

BOY'S O——KAY.

The Dogface Soldier

This was a popular song that kept our spirits up

D: WWII Casualties

For those who have wondered when and where their division was formed, who the assigned and attached units were, the past campaigns, and how the division stacked up against other units in their theater, there is a massive reference book that is worth reading. The book is "Order of Battle, U.S. Army, World War II", by Captain Shelby Stanton. Published in 1984 by the Presidio Press, Novato, CA, the book covers the status of the Army before WWII, the activation, redesignation, phasing in and phasing out that took place on a continual basis before, during, and after the war. Infantry, Armored, and Cavalry Divisions are covered as well as Regiments, Battalions (Infantry, Airborne, Artillery, Armor, Tank Destroyers, Coast Artillery, Anti-Aircraft Artillery, Engineers, and other special units). It is a massive reference that accurately traces all of these units. The casualty lists do not include MIAs but they are based on unit records and this reference has DA approval. Incidentally, there is a similar version published for Vietnam and one is in the works for Korea.

In looking at these 89 major units, the statistics contain a number of stories worth telling:

• The 3rd Infantry Division ("Rock of the Marne", "Marne Division") participated in 10 campaigns including the invasions of North Africa, Sicily, Anzio, and Southern France, 531 combat days; more casualties than any other division (24,334 KIA, WIA, died of wounds); 34 Medals of Honor.

• The 32nd Infantry Division (the "Iron Brigade" of the Civil War) that started combat with a 150 mile march over the Owen Stanley Mountains and ended up with more than 600 days of combat—the most of any American Division.

• The last Infantry Division ("The Big Red One", "Fighting First") was the oldest Regular Army division entering the war. It fought through 8 campaigns from North Africa, Sicily, and Omaha Beach, Aachen, the Bulge, and the major Rhine crossing.

• The National Guard did it's job well: 8 of the 20 Infantry Divisions in Europe with 10,000 casualties or more were Guard units and 10 of 22 divisions in the Pacific were from the Guard.

• The Armored Divisions paid a steep price for their hard fighting: the 1st and 2nd participated in 7 campaigns; the 3rd had over 9,000 casualties, the 10th Armored had over 3800 casualties.

• One Division was wiped out: the Philippine Division which battled the Japanese to the very end on Bataan.

• One new division, the 106th Infantry, lost 6,697 POWs at the start of the Bulge.

• The Airborne divisions in Europe also suffered heavily as airborne operations led the way in Sicily, Italy, Normandy, and Holland. The 82nd's 6 campaigns and 8,511 casualties is followed closely by the 101st's 4 campaigns and 8,478 casualties, with the 17th just behind with 6286 casualties. The 11th Airborne drop on Corregidor and it's brutal fight for Manilla cost the division 2,540 casualties.

This, then, is the list of casualties suffered by the major infantry and armored units in Europe and the Pacific. The list does not include MIAs.

Europe: Armored Divisions

Unit	Campaigns	KIA	WIA	Died of Wounds	Total
1. 3rd Armored Div.	5	1,810	8.963	316	9,089
2. 1st Amtorad Div.	7	1,194	5.169	234	6,596
3. 4th Armored Div.	4	1,143	4.551	213	5,907
4. 2nd Armored Div.	7	981	4,557	202	5,740
5. 7th Armored Div.	4	898	3,811	200	4,909
6. 6th Armored Div.	5	833	3,668	156	4,655
7. 5th Armored Div.	5	570	2,442	140	3,985
6. 10th Armored Div.	2	842	3,109	132	3,883
9. 12th Armored Div.	3	816	2,416	109	3,141
10. 9th Armored Div.	3	570	2,280	123	2,973
11. 11th Armored Div.	3	432	2,394	90	2,916
12. 14th Armored Div.	3	505	1,955	55	2,515
13. 8th Armored Div.	3	393	1,572	73	2,038
14. 13th Armored Div.	2	214	912	39	1,165
15. 20th Armored Div.	1	46	134	13	193
16. 16th Armored Div.	1	4	28	1	33

Europe: Airborne Divisions

Unit	Campaigns	KIA	WIA	Died of Wounds	Total
1. 82nd Abn. Div.	6	1,619	6,560	332	8,511
2. 101st Abn. Div.	4	1,766	6,388	324	8,476
3. 17th Abn.Div.	3	1,191	4,904	191	6,286
4. 13th Abn. Div.	1	-	-	-	-

Europe: Mountain Division

Unit	Campaigns	KIA	WIA	Died of Wounds	Total
1. 10th Mtn. Div.	2	872	3,134	81	4,087

129

Europe: Infantry Divisions

Unit	Campaigns	KIA	WIA	Died of Wounds	Total
1. 3rd Inf. Div.	10	4,922	18.766	636	24,334
2. 4th Inf. Div.	5	4.097	17,371	757	22,225
3. 9th Inf. Div.	9	3.856	17,416	646	21,920
4. 29th Inf. Div.	4	3.887	15,541	899	20,327
5. 1st Inf. Div.	8	3.816	15,208	564	19.488
6. 45th Inf. Div.	5	3.547	14,441	533	18.521
7. 90th Inf. Div.	5	3.342	14,386	588	18,316
8. 30th Inf. Div	5	3.003	13,376	513	16.892
9. 36th Inf. Div	7	3,131	13.191	506	16.828
10. 2nd Inf. Div.	5	3,031	12.785	457	16,272
11. 90th Inf. Div.	4	3,038	12.484	442	15,964
12. 83rd Inf. Div.	5	3,161	11.607	459	15,427
13. 34th Inf. Div.	6	2,866	11,545	464	14.815
14. 35th Inf. Div.	5	2,485	11,526	462	14,473
15. 79th Inf. Div.	5	2,476	10.971	467	13,914
16. 9th Inf. Div.	4	2,532	10.057	288	12,877
17. 28th Inf. Div.	5	2.316	9,609	367	12,292
18. 5th Inf. Div.	5	2.298	9.549	358	12,205
19. 88th Inf. Div.	3	2.248	9.225	258	11,731
20. 26th Inf. Div.	4	1.850	7,866	262	9,998
21. 91st Inf. Div.	3	1,400	6.748	178	8,323
22. 85th Inf. Div.	3	1,561	8,314	175	8.050
23. 78th Int. Div.	3	1.427	6,103	193	7,728
24. 84th Inf. Div,	3	1,284	5.098	154	6,536
25. 95th Inf. Div,	4	1,205	4,945	167	6,317
26. 94th Inf. Div.	4	1,009	4,789	147	5,945
27. 87th Inf. Div.	3	1,154	4,342	141	5.637
28. 44th Inf. Div.	3	1,038	4.209	168	5.415
29. 99th Inf. Div.	3	993	4.177	141	5.311
30. 104th Inf. Div.	3	971	3,657	143	4.771
31. 102nd Inf. Div.	2	932	3,668	145	4.745
32. 100th Inf. Div.	3	883	3.539	101	4.523
33. 63rd Inf. Div.	2	861	3.326	113	4,300
34. 75th Inf. Div.	3	817	3,314	111	4,242
35. 103rd Inf. Div.	3	720	3,329	101	4,150
36. 70th Inf. Div.	2	755	2,713	79	3,547
37. 42nd Inf. Div.	2	553	2,212	85	2.850
36. 92nd Inf. Div. (c)	2	548	2.187	63	2,803
39. 76th Inf. Div.	3	433	1,811	93	2,334
40. 106th Inf. Div.	3	417	1,278	53	1.748**
41. 69th Inf. Div.	2	341	1,146	42	1,529
42. 66th Inf. Div	1	795	836	5	1,436
43. 65th Inf. Div.	2	233	927	27	1,187
44. 71st Inf. Div.	2	243	843	35	1,121
45. 89th Inf. Div.	2	292	692	33	1,017
46. 97th Inf. Div.	1	188	721	26	935
47. 86th Inf. Div.	1	136	618	25	779

130

Unit	Campaigns	KIA	WIA	Died of Wounds	Total
1. 7th Inf. Div.	4	1,948	7,258	386	9,592
2. 96th Inf. Div.	2	1.563	7,181	473	9.217
3. 77th Inf. Div.	3	1,449	5,935	401	7.785
4. 32nd Inf. Div.	3	1,613	5,627	372	7.612
S. 24th Inf. Div.	5	1.374	5,621	315	7,210
6. 27th Inf. Div.	3	1.512	4,960	332	6,824
7. 43rd Inf. Div.	4	1.128	4,887	278	6,293
8. 37th Inf. Div.	2	1.094	4,861	250	6,205
9. 25th Inf. Div.	4	1,235	4,190	262	5,687
10. 41st Inf. Div.	3	743	3,504	217	4,464
11. 1st Cav. Div.	5	734	3,311	236	4,281
12. American Div.	4	981	3,052	176	4,209
13. 38th Inf. Div.	3	645	2,914	139	3,598
14. 40th Inf. Div.	3	614	2,407	134	3,155
15. 33rd Inf. Div.	2	396	2,024	128	2,546
16. 81st Inf. Div.	2	366	1,942	149	2,457
17. 6th Inf. Div.	2	410	1,957	104	2,471
18. 31st Inf. Div.	1	340	1,392	74	1,805
19. 93rd Inf. Div. (c)	3	12	121	5	138
20. 98th Inf. Div.	·	·	·	·	·
21. Phillipine Div.	1	?	?	?	?*

Notation on tables:

(c) = Colored (African-American)

* = Philippine Div. Suffered heavy losses during fall of 1942. Destroyed as a division. Casualties are undetermined

** = 5697 POWs for the 106th Inf. Div. during Battle of the Bulge

132

Made in the USA
Monee, IL
18 September 2023

42916552R00077